T0194781

REGULATION
— FROM THE —
INSIDE OUT:
LINKING YOUR BODY, BRAIN, AND BEHAVIOR

Carolen A. Hope, PhD

BALBOA.PRESS
A DIVISION OF HAY HOUSE

Balboa Press books may be ordered through booksellers or by contacting:

Balboa Press
A Division of Hay House
1663 Liberty Drive
Bloomington, IN 47403
www.balboapress.com
844-682-1282

Because of the dynamic nature of the Internet, any web addresses or links contained in this book may have changed since publication and may no longer be valid. The views expressed in this work are solely those of the author and do not necessarily reflect the views of the publisher, and the publisher hereby disclaims any responsibility for them.

The author of this book does not dispense medical advice or prescribe the use of any technique as a form of treatment for physical, emotional, or medical problems without the advice of a physician, either directly or indirectly. The intent of the author is only to offer information of a general nature to help you in your quest for emotional and spiritual well-being. In the event you use any of the information in this book for yourself, which is your constitutional right, the author and the publisher assume no responsibility for your actions.

Any people depicted in stock imagery provided by Getty Images are models, and such images are being used for illustrative purposes only. Certain stock imagery © Getty Images.

Print information available on the last page.

ISBN: 979-8-7652-4259-9 (sc)
ISBN: 979-8-7652-4261-2 (hc)
ISBN: 979-8-7652-4260-5 (e)

Library of Congress Control Number: 2023909909

Balboa Press rev. date: 06/21/2023

For my mother
Mathilda Frances Sanders
A life of faith, service, and acceptance.

And for my husband Steve, with love.

CONTENTS

INTRODUCTION

Regulation plays a critical role in our ability to express ourselves in healthy ways. A regulated nervous system is the foundation for positive engagement, learning, and resilience. The ability to self-regulate affects our physical states, energy levels, attention, emotions, and behavior. Well-regulated people are more likely to respond than react, to form healthy relationships, to meet challenges effectively, and to deal with challenging behaviors.

Staying regulated is like having an effective internal manager. We are better able to listen, accurately process information, and be compassionate. We can talk with those who have a different viewpoint and solve problems together, and we act in ways that are pro-self and pro-social. In short, a well-regulated nervous system is key to a happy and successful life.

On the other hand, a brain and body system that is prone to dysregulation is a liability (Stein and Kendall 2014). Dysregulation disrupts developing mind-body systems and leads to ongoing negative emotions and behaviors. Problems staying regulated become the basis for chronic negative patterns. One of the most important tasks we can undertake is to help children learn to self-regulate. Adults can teach, model, and remediate regulation skills in order to give children a chance to learn and thrive.

Regulation and the Mind-Body System

Physical state: relaxed, loose versus rigid, tense

Energy level: calm, flexible versus drained, manic

Attention: focused, directed versus distracted, hyper-focused

Emotions: fluid, responsive versus disconnected, overwhelmed, out of control

Behavior: pro-self, pro-social versus self-destructive, other-destructive

It is important to recognize that adults often assume that children should be able to regulate themselves. However, some children have not yet acquired these skills (DelaHooke 2019). For others, especially children who demonstrate serious disruptive or destructive behaviors, a dysregulated nervous system may be habitual. The good news is that advances in science have deepened our understanding of how the brain develops, learns, and regulates. With this knowledge, it is now possible to impact directly the systems that help or hinder self-control.

This book uses a science-practice approach. It presents scholarly content in an accessible manner, then offers relevant activities and experiences aimed at strengthening regulation skills. The material has a strong foundation in brain science, and is consistent with the perspective that dysregulated behavior reflects skill deficits rather than character deficits. As such, dysregulation can be influenced directly due the brain's neuroplasticity and the body's ability to change in response to experience.

Working with challenging behavior can undermine any adult's sense of safety, competence, and worth. It becomes easy to blame the child or system or to believe that "nothing works."

Instead, this volume aims to give hope to educators, counselors, and specialists working with difficult, dangerous, or at-risk youth, and to offer a direction forward.

Organization and Structure

The first chapters review some of the basic principles that underlie behavior change and provide a foundation for the next section, which explores specific brain-body systems that are pathways for increasing or decreasing regulation. The content chapters end with a reflection exercise to help the reader integrate new material and increase awareness around personal attitudes, beliefs, or behaviors that themselves can be problematic to staying regulated. Activity and intervention chapters follow and include experiences and exercises for children, activities for all ages, and resources for adults.

For simplicity's sake, this book will use the terms vertical brain, horizontal brain, and social brain as a way to identify the brain systems. It uses these labels to describe the three distinct brain structures with their associated processes and needs because the terms are easy to remember and they mirror the physical locations of the brain parts.

For example, the vertical brain and its stress response system is on a vertical axis, the hemispheres are located next to one another on a horizontal plane, and the social brain's engagement circuits connect people. When we are able to identify or distinguish which particular system is activated during dysregulation, we can choose an appropriate intervention. Knowing how each system can become a regulation pathway guides the intervention process.

Chapter 1 defines regulation and contrasts it with dysregulation. It takes a look at the stress response system and how early experiences can undermine the ability to self-regulate. The discussion explores the relationship between toxic stress and the development of chronic dysfunctional behavior patterns. It examines the impact of toxic stress on brain development and explains how toxic stress is implicated in maladaptive coping strategies.

The second chapter investigates how the brain changes for better or for worse. This is neuroplasticity's light and dark sides. Chapter 2 presents research on the essential role that sustained attention plays in learning. Sustained attention leads to positive change, laying the groundwork for the targeted intervention process. These research findings become the foundation for a sense of renewed possibility for addressing regulation deficits.

Chapter 3 has over a dozen activities that can be effective tools in strengthening regulatory control regardless of which of the three pathways is activated. These strategies and techniques are based in movement and exercise, mindfulness, and breath and energy. They can be applied in a variety of settings, are often fast-acting, and have wide-ranging applicability for restoring and strengthening regulation.

Movement or exercise is a powerful regulator because it brings immediate change to brain wave states, thoughts, feelings, and moods. The experiences that change our physical states uplift our emotions, help develop executive functioning, and improve problem-solving skills.

Mindfulness or mindful awareness practices are increasingly popular self-help tools that reduce stress levels, improve mood, and increase life satisfaction. The benefits of mindfulness and learning to gain acceptance of the present moment are well-researched and beneficial for both physical and psychological well-being.

Breath- and energy-related techniques increase the capacity to calm the body and soothe the mind. These techniques are based in disciplines like yoga and acupressure, and offer helpful ways to combat the effects of chronic stress. The next section introduces the three brain systems, explores their roles as regulation pathways, and provides dozens of related activities.

Three Regulation Pathways

Dysregulation involves different brain structures, occurs for different reasons, and taps into specific human needs. For these reasons, each of the three brain systems has its own unique strategies and experiences that work best for that pathway. For example, talking things out is calming during a horizontal system meltdown. But dialogue can escalate dysregulation when the vertical brain is triggered during the stress response. Relevant activities follow each system chapter in a chapter of their own.

Chapters 4 and 5 focus on the vertical brain. The vertical brain is probably the system most often associated with regulation problems and it is linked to current issues like trauma-informed programming, toxic stress, and school safety. These chapters explore how the stress response system is activated, and how negative stress response patterns develop and affect regulation.

When integrated, the vertical brain uses higher-level thinking skills to solve problems, manage emotions, and experience well-being. When threatened, higher-level thinking becomes unavailable, integration ceases, and a child moves into a "life or death" defensive stance.

Several of the experiences included in Chapter 5, "Vertical Activities," target skills that deal with the stress response, mind-body connection, and emotional intelligence. Adults who recognize how safety impacts regulation deal more effectively with internal and external threats and adjust their communication styles accordingly. They may have pre-arranged tools or techniques for the dysregulated child to access easily. These adults are usually skilled at noticing when they themselves are triggered.

Chapters 6 and 7 explore the horizontal brain, the hemispheres, and the specialization processes that take place over time. Each hemisphere is home to unique abilities, specific types of knowledge, performance skills, and perspectives. Hemisphere strengths and weaknesses affect cognitive (thinking) and affective (feeling) styles, information processing, and problem solving. Hemisphere strengths and weaknesses shape our personalities and can even become biases, limiting the ways that we see others and express our values.

Regardless of intellectual, physical, or emotional differences, everyone has a need to feel valued and valuable. When adults recognize their own biases, they have the opportunity to create environments where every child is appreciated no matter his or her hemisphere strengths and weaknesses. When a child's way of seeing the world is validated, the child relaxes, feels seen, and stays regulated.

The "Horizontal Activities" chapter includes skill-building exercises to broaden awareness of strengths and weaknesses, strengthen brain-based wellness, and increase complementarity and balance. Balance or complementarity aims to strengthen the ability to solve complex problems and enrich engagement with the world.

The brain is a social organ that uses interactions and relationships to learn about itself, others, and the world. Chapters 8 and 9 highlight the social brain's engagement system and mirror neuron network. Connection is a deep-seated human need and specialized brain cells fire in response to the actions and mental states of other people to help us understand their behavior and intentions. Relationships become sources of comfort throughout one's lifetime.

There is a dark side to the social engagement system. Early destructive relationships prime children toward dysregulation. Social misperception and negative engagement patterns become the norm as early toxic experiences lead to sensitivity to other people's dysregulation. Feeling disconnected or unacceptable often leads to isolation, withdrawal, or aggression.

The social engagement network is an interpersonal resource system that helps us form and sustain meaningful relationships. The "Social Activities" chapter includes experiences to lessen the consequences of adverse early experiences, explores the process of emotional contagion, and moves to strengthen social emotional learning. Savvy adults use techniques that foster relationships, and that encourage responsiveness rather than reactivity. They emphasize connection over conformity, and provide corrective experiences that help children grow beyond what they have known.

Regulation Pathways and Human Needs

Vertical system: Need to be secure and to feel safe

Horizontal system: Need to be valued and to feel seen

Social engagement system: Need to affiliate and feel accepted

---

The final chapter summarizes core concepts and invites the reader to re-think problematic behavior, conceptualizing it by using the three-systems model. It revisits the significance of early and ongoing developmental trauma and the needs that drive patterns of dysregulation. Chapter 10 invites the reader to reflect on his or her own regulation patterns and to invest in new ways of considering and being with problem behaviors. The discussion recapitulates the encouraging perspective that even in the most extreme cases, targeted interventions create a possibility for change.

This book has some limitations that deserve mentioning. First, there was a deliberate attempt to simplify complex brain concepts in order to make the material and models more accessible. The author apologies for any confusion or distortion. Next, there are many significant external factors that also have a profound influence on regulation. These were not discussed solely because they were beyond the scope of this project.

CHAPTER 1

REGULATION, STRESS, AND POSSIBILITY

Self-regulation is the ability to manage energy, emotion, attention, and behavior in ways that are appropriate and consistent with a person's goals. Regulation is an important part of healthy self-expression, and many factors underlie the ability to be regulated, including brain development, physical health, mental fitness, social connectedness, and trauma history.

Regulating emotions and behavior is a dynamic interplay of body, brain, thoughts, emotions, and action systems. Well-regulated expression is pro-social and meaningful. Thoughts, feelings, and actions make sense and fit the moment. Dysregulated expressions fail to align with self-interest and neither fit the situation nor serve the betterment of others.

Moving toward Holism

Having a regulated nervous system is essential to our well-being. When we are able to self-regulate, we express ourselves in ways that help us grow, learn, and connect with others. We are able to resist unhealthy strategies to cope with and manage uncomfortable feelings and impulses. Our mind and body systems, internal and external expressions, are coordinated and organized wholes.

Regulation underlies all behavior, and it is essential that we consider this when working with difficult children. When we assess a child's emotional and behavioral challenges in terms of regulatory control, it is possible to be more curious and less judgmental. We begin to take into account the child's development, early history, current needs, and available resources. This is a move from a model of character deficit to a model of brain- and body-skill deficit, and an attempt to move away from a value judgment.

Without this shift in perception, it is easy to view a child as disobedient or defective. Labels like "troublemaker" or "oppositional" come to mind. These reinforce the sense that the child is bad, flawed, or unredeemable, and foreclose on many opportunities for positive interaction and change.

A regulation-based model of behavior moves us from pathology to possibility. With this perspective, challenging behaviors occur, but they reflect deficits in regulatory capacity rather than deliberate willfulness. Our responses become more attuned and effective as we address destructive cognitive, emotional, and physiological patterns through targeted intervention planning.

Regulation versus Dysregulation

When dysregulation occurs, sensations, thoughts, feelings, and behaviors are not aligned with well-being, are destructive toward others, and fall outside the norm. To illustrate, imagine a model like the bell-shaped curve representing all the individual behaviors that might occur in any situation. Well-regulated behaviors would be in the center of the curve, while the dysregulated reactions would be in one of the bell curve's two tails. These behaviors are outliers that differ significantly from what is expected or considered acceptable.

Examples might include being aggressive and dangerous on one hand or withdrawn and self-injurious on the other. Dysregulated reactions do more harm than good but can bring a momentary sense of relief, even when they are inappropriate or destructive (Fisher 2017). Dysregulation discharges negative feelings and can be a distraction from uncomfortable thoughts or sensations.

We use the term *dysregulation* loosely and in several ways. When we notice escalating behavior problems, we might say that a child is becoming dysregulated. Or we might notice that we seem out of sync with our thoughts or feelings and describe this sense as being dysregulated.

Many factors underlie the ability to stay regulated, and the next section will explore one of the main challenges to this critical process: the stress response.

Cultural Awareness

Be aware of cultural differences in emotional and behavioral norms like individual and unique ways to celebrate, acknowledge, and express strong emotions; use physical space; demonstrate closeness; or engage in conflict.

The term *dysregulation* is helpful when used to describe a mind-body state or a lack of skill mastery. It is not meant to impose a dominant view on what actions and feelings should look like.

Responding to Stress

When threatened, our brains mobilize in order to protect us. In an instant, the emotional brain activates a series of chemical-change events that initiate the stress response and create physical and physiological states aimed at survival. In most cases, when the threat subsides, the reactions pass, and the brain and body systems return to normal.

This activation of the stress response system, commonly known as fight or flight, also includes the states of freeze and faint. These latter states are based in submitting rather than acting, but they also serve to preserve us and keep us safe. To illustrate, when a tiger approaches, you could fight or you could run. But you might also stay still and try to be invisible, or play dead to keep from being devoured.

Each individual reacts to stress in unique ways. When threatened, one child might become aggressive and hit or kick, whereas another child might cry or run. A different child might become spacey or tune out, and another might stand frozen, unable even to speak. Despite these dramatically different expressions, similar brain and body systems are being activated.

Stress responses are adaptive when they are appropriate to the situation and when they are relieved in a timely manner. It is understandable to feel frustration or momentary irritation when faced with an unexpected obstacle or challenge. It can be helpful to shut down or tune out after being overstimulated by noise or activity. Once the situation is managed or addressed, readjustment should follow. For the average person, these mind and body changes wind down after a threat passes.

However, ongoing threats to safety, identity, and well-being can become pathways to emotional and behavioral regulation problems. *A chronically activated stress response system primes a child for dysregulation, becoming a reactive pattern whether a situation is threatening or not.* When a child faces unrelenting challenges and threats, the stress response can turn into a default setting.

Ongoing dysregulation decreases a child's ability to learn and interferes with positive growth and development (Lieberman and Van Horn 2011). Early and ongoing negative experiences create toxic stress. Toxic stress can lead to permanent developmental deficits and chronic negative regulation and response patterns. The next section examines how this happens and what the effects might look like.

Toxic Stress and Brain Development

Dealing with stress is an important part of early development, and children need to explore novel situations. During an unfamiliar or uncomfortable experience, it is natural for the stress response system to activate. Meeting a stranger, being in a new environment, or eating an unusual food triggers the stress response system and sends stress chemicals through the brain and body.

When caring adults help a child work through these minor stressors, they soothe and protect the child with a word or touch, and stress levels taper off. As a result, a child's regulation ability develops, resilience is optimized, and the brain areas dedicated to skill development, learning, and connection are strengthened. However, in the absence of a caring response, the stress response system stays activated, and as a result, a child experiences toxic stress. *Toxic stress is the chronic activation of the stress response system in children and adults.*

Toxic stress can put the stress response system permanently on high alert, producing chronic destructive emotional and behavioral patterns. The patterns develop as stressed brains reinforce or strengthen the neural pathways dedicated to carrying stress-related signals. In time these pathways develop at the expense of other more positive brain regions. The patterns can be intense, long-lasting, and unpredictable, and result in lifelong difficulty with learning, coping, and self-mastery (Schore 2015).

The consequences of toxic stress have been directly related to academic challenges, stress-related symptoms and illness, and dysregulation. In other words, stress-laden brain networks diminish the skills associated with memory, learning, executive functioning, and regulation (Blaustein and Kinniburgh 2018).

Dysfunction in the home and family is the most common source of toxic stress. Many children live in hazardous settings or in homes affected by financial insecurity, addiction, violence, and abuse. Statistics on child neglect themselves are sobering and show that a high percentage of school-age children experience toxic stress in their living situations. In the presence of these kinds of experiences, a child's stress response system stays activated, decreasing his or her potential for successfully navigating many of life's demands.

Adverse Childhood Experiences (ACEs)

The ACE study of the 1990s identified the kind of early experiences that significantly influence later lifestyle and health behavior choices (Felitti et al. 1998).

Ten experiences associated with abuse, neglect, and household dysfunction were found to correlate strongly with academic failure, poor mental health, substance abuse, and mortality. Having only three ACEs can make a serious difference in the trajectory of a child's life.

Toxic stress is a key factor that affects many regulation pathways. When stress is not relieved in a short time frame, it overwhelms developing systems, changing brain structures and functions. Fortunately, many of these changes can be reversed using targeted brain- and body-based interventions. The next chapter will take a look at the brain's amazing ability to heal, grow, and regain lost skills through its unique property of neuroplasticity.

Main Ideas

When we are able to regulate our energy levels, attention, emotions, and behaviors, we express ourselves in individual, healthy, and pro-social ways. By using a regulation model to understand challenging behaviors, we come at them from a more inclusive and holistic perspective. We leave labeling or pathologizing behind and recognize the complex systems and dynamics that help us make sense of a child's destructive behaviors.

The stress response system is an intricate survival mechanism by which we recognize and react to perceived danger. Each of us mobilizes against threats in individual ways drawing from the reactions of fight, flight, freeze, and faint.

Even positive experiences can be stressful, and it is important that nurturing adults help children accommodate new experiences. When children successfully manage stressful experiences, they gain critical skills in areas like learning, attention, and self-regulation.

Toxic stress can prevent a young brain from acquiring important skills and learning to calm itself and downregulate. As the brain remains on high alert, a default setting results. This setting becomes a key factor in behavior, the observable response to our internal and external experiences. Toxic stress is linked to many of the physical, emotional, and behavioral symptoms we observe in dysregulated children.

Reader Reflection

The scientist-practitioner model is an educational perspective dedicated to the practical application of scholarly knowledge. This book is based on this model, meaning that when we act as scientist-practitioners, we acquire new information and techniques, reflect on current practices, integrate ongoing scholarship, and update our technologies. Whether we are educators, specialists, or interested adults, we benefit by active introspection and engagement (Whitaker 2012).

The Reflection exercises are meant to encourage the reader to evaluate the personal beliefs and experiences that influence your work with children. You may be asked to examine assumptions, define unfamiliar terms, consider ways to apply new information to a problem, use a rating scale, or participate in a thought experiment.

Consider the following

Begin by entering a reflective state using a favorite method, like quieting your body, slowing your breath, or softening your gaze.

- When kids act out, what do you believe about their behavior? Why do they do what they do?
- Can you make a positive change in a child's behavior?
- In your role as _____ (educator, specialist, parent), whose job is it to help children change?

Choose a child or situation that has been troubling or challenging. Maybe it is a child who wakes you or keeps you up at night. You worry about safety issues or the trajectory of their life choices. Notice any thoughts, images, or feelings in your body.

- What is most difficult about this person/situation?
- Do you feel hopeful or hopeless?
- How does the situation/problem affect you?

Get specific about this challenge.

- What factors "set things up" or "get things going"?
- Can you predict trouble or "see" it coming?
- What have you tried to keep things from escalating?
- What makes things worse?

Consider the information about regulation, the stress response, and toxic stress.

- How does regulation impact the situation?
- Does toxic stress play a role in the difficulties?
- Does your own stress response contribute to the problem?

Rating Scales

Rating scales can help clarify how something affects us in the present moment. They are informal devices that increase awareness about a person, situation, or event by measuring its impact. Rating scales organize and create boundaries around difficult emotional experiences and help us notice trends and track changes over time.

Consider the experience you chose for this reflection. How much distress do you feel about the child or situation in this moment?

Rate the experience from 0 to 10, where 0 means something like, "I feel great about this," or "No problem." A score of 10 means "This is one of the most disturbing people or situations I deal with," or "I feel completely overwhelmed by this."

Notice what you say to yourself as you rate your distress.

CHAPTER 2

NEUROPLASTICITY AND THE REGULATION PATHWAYS

Early negative experiences and toxic stress hinder brain development and result in skill deficits and chronic patterns of dysregulation. While it is not possible to turn back the clock on early trauma, scientists and educators can address developmental deficits and maladaptive patterns with targeted interventions (Jensen 2005).

Targeted interventions are games, exercises, and activities designed to improve attention and concentration, support healthy engagement, and enhance learning. Brain-based interventions can even strengthen empathy and compassion. How do we create these change tools, and how do we know that they work?

Neuroplasticity's Light and Dark Sides

Targeted brain development and change relies on a unique quality of the brain called neuroplasticity, the brain's ability to change over time. Just as plastic can be shaped or molded, the brain responds to new experiences by changing its shape and function. Experiences change what the brain looks like and what it can do because the brain constantly rewires itself by adding or pruning connections.

To illustrate, the brain has about 100 billion brain cells, or neurons. Each brain cell has about 10,000 connections to other neurons. When a neuron is active, it "fires," and grows its connections, as if it were forming a network or web. The connections create circuits. Each circuit relates to the particular kind of mental activity that is happening in that moment, such as perceiving sights or sounds, moving, or using abstract thought and reasoning. The more a specific circuit is activated, the stronger it becomes. It's like exercising to stay fit.

Neuroplasticity can work against children who experience ongoing abuse or neglect, or whose early development was derailed by toxic stress. These brains have strengthened or reinforced the neural pathways dedicated to carrying stress-related signals, and negative life experiences continue to influence the ability to regulate, learn, and connect. These children are often inattentive, disinterested, or noncompliant, and their behavior may be distracting or dangerous in the classroom or in public settings. This is the dark side of neuroplasticity (Porges 2011).

While we cannot roll back time, we can help the brain rewire itself in positive ways. Brain-based strategies and tools can address developmental failures, improve self-control, and increase readiness to learn. Even dangerous and disruptive patterns improve through time. Some basic neuroscience can help illustrate how this is possible (Jensen 2009).

Focused Attention: Precursor to Change

Each person's brain has a physical size and shape based on factors like genetics, health, lifestyle choices, and experiences. Each brain also manifests a unique set of strengths and weaknesses, skills, preferences, and abilities. Just as an athlete will train in order to perform certain skilled feats, the brain can also "flex its muscles" and develop specific attributes and strengths. It does this through the process of deliberate attention. *Attention and activity change brain structure and function.*

A vital way the brain "works out" is by paying attention, focusing, and remembering. As stated earlier, repeated and ongoing activation of a circuit strengthens its connections, growing the brain. In other words, as neurons fire, they grow their networks. As scientists like to say, "Neurons that fire together, wire together."

When we focus our attention, repeated and ongoing activation takes place. *Focused attention is sustained, deliberate attention that results in acquiring new mental skills.* Focused attention uses intention and effort as it molds the brain. By directing our attention, we create an experience that changes both the brain's shape and what it can do.

Neuroimaging plays a central role in letting us know that the brain can change. Neuroimaging tools produce pictures of brain structures and activities, and are able to show what is happening in the brain in real time. With technologies like functional magnetic resonance imaging (fMRI), or computerized tomography (CAT) scans, it is possible to observe and measure the brain in the present moment and over the course of time. Scientists can answer questions like whether an intervention has reached its target area or has had a desired effect (Rakesh and Whittle 2021).

For example, scientists used fMRIs to examine the brains of professional violinists (Jäncke 2009). They found that the musicians' brains had larger and more developed regions in the front part of brain, known as the frontal cortex. These enlarged areas are associated with the left hand, the hand that generates each individual note on the violin. Repeated practice (i.e., focused attention) had produced changes in the brains' shape and performance.

Another research project included children who learned the fundamentals of playing the piano (Rauscher et. al. 1997). Researchers found that these children's brains became significantly different from those of their peers. The regions associated with spatial temporal reasoning, skills for accurate location in space and time, were more developed. There were even long-term changes in abilities relating to mathematics and science.

In another study, children participated in a short mindfulness training (de Bruin et al. 2014). The group used focused attention during their practice, and after several weeks, they showed stronger scores on measures of happiness, self-regulation, and quality of life. The subjects were also rated higher in "present-moment non-judgmental awareness."

Focused attention helps the brain develop and mature in healthy ways, and self-regulation skills are essential for focused attention. Strong self-regulation means a child can work at doing and being his or her best, and can reach out to others when needing help. The ability to self-regulate helps children calm down when they are upset and cheer up when they are down.

Regulation either underpins or undermines positive change and therefore deserves the full attention of educators and related specialists (Bashant 2020). *Regulation is a critical component in focused attention and is necessary for the brain-based techniques that move children beyond their history of toxic stress.*

For many adults who work with children, regulation issues have remained hidden in the management of emotional and behavioral acting out. It has been common to identify the child or the behavior as the problem and to then choose among a limited repertoire of compliance-based solutions. While these techniques may be somewhat effective, they presuppose an inherent ability to meet certain behavioral standards. This ability may or may not be available to the child.

Regulation-based interventions target and strengthen deficits. They may, for example, teach children to manage their energy levels, relax their bodies, or direct their attention. These changes have lasting benefits. The next section will explore the benefit of a regulation-based perspective and briefly introduce three regulation pathways.

Targeted Change and the Regulation Pathways

The vertical brain, the horizontal brain, and the social engagement system are three brain and body systems that are linked to regulation. These systems can become pathways for either increasing or decreasing regulation. The pathway model was created to organize how we think about children's behavior, and to guide the interactions and interventions that optimize engagement and learning.

The Three Regulation Pathways

The Vertical Brain
Optimal state is integration.
The child asks, "Am I safe?"
Wants the adult to protect him or her and remain calm.

The Horizontal Brain
Optimal state is balance and complementarity.
The child asks, "Am I seen?"
Wants the adult to value him or her and be inclusive.

The Social Brain
Optimal state is connection.
The child asks, "Am I accepted?"
Wants the adult to relate to him or her and foster belonging.

The vertical brain system is housed near the brain's central vertical axis. The stress response system is an important part of this system, whose emphasis is the need for safety and security. *When we feel safe, the vertical brain stays regulated and dampens the impulses to fight, flee, freeze, or faint.*

When regulated, the vertical brain smoothly manages higher-level skills and expressions, including thoughts (cognition), feelings (affect and emotions), and actions (behaviors). Thoughts inform and help shape our feelings, and feelings guide our reasoning and update thinking. At the same time, the body provides support and a strong, congruent foundation for these complex processes.

Toxic stress disrupts vertical integration. When educators and specialists recognize this, they tune in and are more able to remain calm when children act out in challenging and threatening ways. Adults who are familiar with vertical pathway dysfunctions ensure that their classrooms, environments, and interactions are free from perceived threats or danger.

The horizontal brain system focuses on the brain hemispheres, which are physically located next to one another. Each hemisphere develops dedicated and unique skills and abilities. Hemisphere specialization influences how individuals perceive and engage in the world. *Hemisphere strengths and weaknesses affect how we think, feel, process information, and solve problems.* Increasing hemisphere balance and complementarity strengthen the ability to gain competence, feel confident, and solve complex problems.

When adults understand that there are many ways of learning and knowing, they create environments where children feel valued regardless of hemisphere strengths and weaknesses. Educators who are more inclusive and knowledgeable about neurodiversity celebrate differences. When a child's way of seeing the world is validated, he or she relaxes and feels appreciated and seen.

The social engagement system is the basis for the third pathway. *The human brain is a social organ that uses interactions and relationships to learn about itself, others, and the world.* The social engagement system shapes our capacity to form positive relationships and it is a foundation for resilience. Healthy social engagement means that we are able to join with those who are trustworthy and that we can give and receive nurturance.

When children feel a sense of belonging, they are more likely to remain regulated. Adults who understand this emphasize connection over conformity, even when confronted with challenging behavior. They provide corrective interpersonal experiences that help children grow beyond what they have known. By staying connected and modeling strong engagement skills, adults increase the likelihood of a positive outcome.

Main Ideas

Neuroplasticity is the brain's ability to change in response to experience. Brain changes can be beneficial or destructive. Because of this, we say that neuroplasticity has a light and a dark side.

Toxic stress leads to skill deficits and chronic patterns of dysfunction. Targeted interventions address the deficits associated with toxic stress and can redirect the trajectory of a child's life.

Focused attention is a sustained, deliberate attention process that strengthens specific brain circuitry and helps develop skills and abilities. Successful focused attention requires a regulated body and mind. In other words, regulation is essential in order for children to engage in the interventions that address the fallout from toxic stress.

This book focuses on three brain systems that act as pathways for increased or decreased regulation. The systems are the vertical brain and stress response system, the horizontal brain and hemisphere specialization, and the social brain's interpersonal engagement system. A regulation-pathway perspective guides the intervention process and increases the likelihood of meeting challenging behavior effectively and with compassion.

Reader Reflection

Recall what you have learned about neuroplasticity, neuroimaging, and focused attention, and consider the following questions.

- How does neuroplasticity impact the brain and change behavior?
- What does it mean when we say, "Neurons that fire together, wire together?"
- Why is focused attention important?
- How can neuroimaging help us know when interventions are effective?
- Why do we say there is a light and dark side to neuroplasticity?

Bring to mind the challenging child or situation from the previous reflection.

- How do regulation issues affect each participant?
- Does a regulation-pathways perspective change the way you see your challenging situation?
- Might one of the three pathways impact this situation?
- Are you more or less hopeful about working with this challenge?

Think about the dark side of neuroplasticity and the lasting effects of toxic stress.

- Is early brain development relevant to your child or situation?
- What would you like to know about the child's personal or family history?

CHAPTER 3

REGULATION ACTIVITIES AND EXPERIENCES: MOVEMENT, MINDFULNESS, AND BREATH AND ENERGY

Neuroplasticity has both a light and a dark side. The dark appears when toxic stress exerts its destructive influence on the developing brain. Early and chronic negative experiences derail potentials for healthy behavior and self-expression. The light side asserts itself when the brain changes for good through targeted interventions. Directed activities increase regulation by addressing areas such as mood, attention, impulse control, and resilience.

Neuroplasticity's Promise

By appreciating the brain's ability to change its shape and function over time, educators and specialists can respond to dysregulated behavior with increased skill and compassion.

Research provides evidence that targeted interventions can transform problems that were once viewed as permanent.

The ability to influence early deficits is the bright side of neuroplasticity and its message of hope.

One of the most important goals for children with behavioral difficulties is to learn to self-regulate. But staying regulated is a foundational skill for adults as well. The following strategies, exercises, and resources are tools for strengthening the ability self-regulate. They can be adapted for most age groups and draw from three general areas: movement, mindful awareness, and breath and energy.

Movement: Powerful, Available, and Evidence-Based

Movement is a simple and often overlooked way to strengthen regulation skills. Physical activity does not have to be strenuous to have a profound effect on brain states. Movement has been referred to as the brain's "Zoloft" and "Ritalin" due to its positive influence on attention and mood, and movement activities are known to heighten focus and concentration.

Physical activity affects the brain first, even before it starts building muscle. It can stimulate chemicals that lift mood, and is one of the only evidence-based neurotransmitter change-agents, aside from medication (Ratey 2011). While it is nearly impossible to "think" yourself out of a bad mood, movement can change your feeling state and shift long-standing emotional patterns.

Movement is simply another name for any physical activity, such as walking, running, exercise, playing sports, free-form play, or dance. Most children enjoy moving their bodies because it is fun and gets quick results. Movement can be used to calm or enliven by choosing a tempo, intensity, and level of effort that matches an energy goal.

What Is Mindfulness?

Mindfulness is a level of consciousness associated with a receptive attitude and a relaxed brain. In a state of mindful awareness, the focus is on the present moment rather than planning for the future or worrying about the past. A mindfulness practice is quite different from other endeavors that require self-evaluation or self-improvement. Instead, mindfulness aims for regular practice based on acceptance and non-judgment. Cultivating mindful awareness is a paradoxical process because change happens by accepting whatever comes in the moment.

Studies show that practicing mindfulness has a positive influence on self-control, flexibility, equanimity, and mental clarity. Mindfulness benefits the ability to relate to others and to oneself with kindness, acceptance, and compassion, and it enhances insight, morality, and intuition (Davidson et al. 2003).

Breath and Energy

Techniques like yoga and acupressure work with the breath or the body's subtle electrical energy systems, and are potent ways to downregulate. Acupressure engages the body's meridian systems and yoga links the breath to movement. Related techniques, like diaphragmatic breathing and meridian tapping, engage the parasympathetic nervous system and help the body stay calm.

Shallow breathing limits attention and learning, and has negative consequences for immune functioning and general health. Rapid shallow breathing is linked to increased pulse rate and blood pressure. Learning to deepen the breath helps modify poor breathing habits and supports regulation. The ability to downregulate helps us be more physically, mentally, and emotionally available.

Activity: Movement as Change Agent

Movement is a powerful, evidence-based change agent that has an immediate effect on brain state. Movement increases regulation and can shift long-standing negative patterns. It improves mood, memory, and learning. Complex movement patterns enlist multiple areas in the brain to help develop attention systems (Madigan 2012).

Movement also supports healthy muscles and bones, and reduces pain. Moving more means a healthier body and improved energy and sleep. Movement exercises can be small and simple or bold and complex. We can move almost anytime, and movement is fun.

Try some of the following.

- Complete a mundane task while standing or stretching. For example, create a movement pattern or choose a dance sequence to use while you are on the phone, writing, or doing dishes.
- Schedule frequent short movement breaks with your students, colleagues, or other staff members. These are especially helpful for restoring focus and relieving fatigue.
- Learn a dance step, new exercise, or yoga pose. Incorporate it into your day. Link the new routine to a regularly scheduled activity to help you build a new habit.
- Select a movement leader and have the group follow that person's movements. Experiment with the pace and the size of the gestures. Try using different kinds of music that align with energy goals.
- Work in pairs. Have one person move slowly while the partner tries to mirror him or her. Reverse roles.
- Engage older students by having them create or share complex patterns from social media.

Activity: Core Movements

Core movements are the simple gestures or movements that are the foundation for all activities and mobility. Pushing, pulling, reaching, grasping, and letting go are examples of core movements. Other core movements are moving toward, moving away, controlling, and yielding. By using these movements singly and in combination, we are able to complete complex tasks and to travel through space.

Early negative experiences may disrupt the fluid execution of fundamental movements. When a movement has been prevented or punished, discomfort can develop. As a result, the individual may feel uncomfortable when he or she yields or moves toward, even when these would be natural, given the situation.

> **Examples of Core Movements**
>
> Pushing and pulling
> Turning toward and turning away
> Grasping and letting go
> Moving toward and moving away
> Staying firm and yielding
> Opening up and closing down

Practicing core movements can build a sense of safety and expand the desire to explore the world (Ogden and Fisher 2015).

- Practice the core movements. Notice how each feels and identify any movements that feel uncomfortable or difficult. Which movements feel easy or pleasurable? Entertain a light and relaxed attitude and present-moment awareness.

- Draw from the movements listed above or from others found in the literature on fundamental movement. Combine moves and create a movement pattern or routine. Gently explore whatever comes up.
- Practice core movements in pairs or in a group. Notice what feels different about this. Be sensitive to how these interactions impact others.

Activity: Rhythm Patterns for Brain Development, Attention, and Focus

Rhythmic movement helps the brain develop in important ways. Rhythm supports executive functions: the skills and processes that allow us to begin, monitor, manage, and complete tasks. *Rhythmic activity strengthens attention and focus, influencing both the ability to attend to relevant stimuli and to disregard distractions.* Rhythm patterns also anchor learning and increase problem-solving ability (Koontz 2022).

Rhythm patterns can be simple or complex, use large or small spaces, and integrate objects like a ball or hacky sack. When we toss and catch, important changes take place in the brain. As oxygen increases in the bloodstream, we heighten focus, expand spatial awareness, and strengthen the power to anticipate and predict. Age-appropriate rhythm games and interactions excite our brains' reward systems, which makes them reinforcing as well as beneficial (Hubert 2014).

Create a repertoire of simple or complex patterns using hand clapping, finger snaps, steps, jumps, and accessories like scarves, balls, or other soft objects. Draw from dance, athletics, yoga, and the latest online moves to shift energy levels, relieve stress, unite a group, or just change things up in the moment.

Rhythm Routine

- Tap thighs, clap, alternate finger snaps
- Bend or twist, step out and back
- Quarter turn and repeat

Rhythm Routine

- Circle with right arm, circle with left arm
- Stand (or stretch), reach both arms upward
- Return arms to "prayer position," fold body downward
- Turn and repeat

Choose a pattern that matches your energy goal. If it is time to calm and soothe, choose a low-key pattern that incorporates slow movement with attention. If the intention is to activate and boost alertness, increase movement and use a quick tempo. Start by matching the group's energy level to gain acceptance and get more "buy in" in the moment. With each repetition, modify the pace as you move toward the energy goal.

Activity: Rhythm Patterns and Executive Functioning

Rhythmic and repetitive movement patterns benefit executive functioning and improve the skills that help us remember information or complete a project. *Rhythm patterns enhance automaticity, retrieval, and repetition, and help connect the brain's prefrontal cortex and the cerebellum.* Improved executive functioning strengthens working memory, mental flexibility, and self-control (Garland 2014).

Executive functioning skills include:

- Self-monitoring;
- Time management;
- Inhibiting impulses;
- Sustaining and shifting attention;
- Cognitive flexibility;
- Emotional control;
- Initiating activity;
- Planning; and
- Organizing time and materials.

Strong executive functioning is critical to success. With these skills, we can set goals, check our progress, meet obstacles, and finish on time. Check the list above.

- Do you see any personal strengths or weaknesses? How do these impact your sense of accomplishment or well-being?
- Target one skill and create an action plan.

Find or create age-appropriate rhythm- and pattern-based games. Make these enjoyable activities a regular part of your day.

Activity: Beginning Mindfulness

Mindfulness practices are based on Buddhist concepts founded about 2,600 years ago. Today, mindfulness is applied in diverse settings, from business to education, yoga studios to hospital clinics. *Although mindfulness has roots in the meditation traditions, we use the term to describe the process of bringing attention to our experiences in the present moment.*

Mindfulness is a brain state that values acceptance of the present moment. When mindful, we relax as the moment unfolds, instead of considering or worrying about the future or about the past. Regular mindfulness practice leads to a calmer body and mind (Kabat-Zin 2009).

Each mindfulness session feels different. Some sessions are easy, some less so; some are peaceful and some are not. The practice of mindfulness decreases reactivity, even when practice itself is difficult or irritating.

Browse the literature on mindfulness. Choose books that are interesting and motivating to you. Share your process or practice with your students, friends, or colleagues.

Mindfulness for Children

Keep mindfulness activities short and simple.
Start slowly and make it interesting.

Rule of thumb: One minute of attention for each year of age. Example: For a child of five, a practice should last about five minutes.

Activity: Mindfulness: Simple or Complex?

Mindfulness practice has far-reaching health benefits. Practicing benefits social, emotional, mental, and physical health. Mindful awareness is an entrance into the mind or inner landscape that provides a "platform" from which to gain clarity and insight.

While mindfulness sounds easy, it is not. The act of directing attention (focused attention) benefits the brain, but keeping the attention anchored can be difficult.

To illustrate, try this "simple" practice.

- Choose to focus on your breath.
- Pay attention to the inhalation and exhalation.
- Notice how long until your attention wanders.
- Notice what kind of experience took your attention away.
- Return to the breath without judgment.

The aim of this practice is to return to the breath over and over, regardless of what occurs. Maybe a string of thoughts takes you far from the present into the past, the future, or the imagined future. Again, return to the breath. Perhaps there is resistance. Again, return to the breath.

Moving Away from the Breath

The following may take you away from the breath.

- What is happening elsewhere in the body
- Thoughts, memories, or feelings
- Rehearsing tasks
- Compiling lists
- Deciding mindfulness is foolish or impossible

Continue to direct and redirect attention without judgment. *Remember that the practice is the progress.* With mindful awareness, attend and notice whatever the mind is doing with self-compassion and kindness.

Activity: Practicing Mindfulness

Mindfulness is associated with a receptive attitude and a brain state consistent with relaxation. Among its benefits are objectivity, tolerance for feelings, and increased emotional intelligence (Hanh 2011). Mindful activities boost willpower and immune functioning, increase self-regulation, and teach us to move from reactivity to receptivity. The effects are known to generalize to many areas of life.

Each mindfulness session is unique and the benefits of practice develop through time. There are endless possibilities for practice. Below are a few simple practices for people of all ages.

I.

- Place both feet on the floor, and sit up straight. Make sure to have a clear airway.
- Notice the body settling down.
- With full attention, watch the sweep of the second hand on the clock, track the path of a cloud, or listen to a piece of music.

II.

- Find an object from nature, such as a flower.
- Direct the attention to the object. Have each person notice when his or her mind wanders and have the person draw it back again.
- After a few minutes, ask each one to share what happened. Listen respectfully and affirm all experiences.

III.

- Strike a bell, singing bowl, or tuning fork.
- Have everyone listen carefully until he or she can no longer hear the tone.

- When the tone has ended, have each person raise his or her hand. Notice that each of us perceives sound differently.
- Have everyone share thoughts and validate all experiences.

Develop a mindfulness practice for yourself so you can anticipate any questions that might arise. Be patient. Share any personal insights.

Activity: Tracking Energy Levels and Well-Being

Using movement in an intentional way can help calm and soothe, wake up alertness, let in, or shake off difficult feelings. An appraisal system or rating scale helps us notice what we are experiencing, in order then to choose a movement that would serve us best. When we have a clear sense of our energy levels and well-being, we can use movements that foster intentional, positive change (Eden and Feinstein 2008).

Consider your energy level.

- Energy can be perceived as a sense of physical, mental, or emotional vitality. Do you feel rested and available, or fatigued? Bored, or involved and engaged? Numb and checked out, or enthusiastically interested?
- Create a scale to capture your impressions. The scale might range from 0 (exhausted) to 10 (exuberant).
- Give yourself a rating. Remember, this is subjective, so there is no wrong answer.
- Let us call this your EL, or Energy Level, score.

Consider your feeling state, welfare, or sense of well-being.

- Do you feel happy, delighted, content, disappointed, or distressed?
- Create a scale to capture your impressions. The scale might range from 0 (hopeless, depressed) to 10 (positive, upbeat).
- Give yourself a rating. Remember, this is a subjective assessment for this moment, not a judgement.
- Let us call this your WB, or Well-Being, score.

Think of an intentional movement, gesture, or pattern that reflects your desired energy level or well-being goal. Do you need more or less activation? Do you need to be uplifted or maintained? Do you need to break or to restore?

- Choose a routine that feels comfortable and that reflects where you are in this moment.

- Practice it for one minute.
- Rest for twenty seconds. Repeat the sequence modifying the tempo and pattern as needed to move toward your goal.
- Repeat the sequence above.

Wait five minutes. Rate yourself using the EL and WB scales.

- Notice any changes. Reflect on resistance, benefits, or problems.

- Consider how your life would be different if you had more energy or a greater sense of well-being.

Activity: Diaphragmatic Breathing

Rapid, shallow breathing is often associated with stress and the stress response. When the amygdala perceives a threat, it sends a signal to the hypothalamus, causing changes that include increased pulse rate, higher blood pressure, and rapid breathing. *The prolonged shallow breathing that accompanies ongoing stress has negative consequences for immune functioning and general health.*

It is possible to change breathing habits by deepening breath using diaphragmatic breathing. Diaphragmatic breathing, sometimes called belly breathing or yoga breath, is a deliberate practice that uses focused attention to deepen breathing gradually. As a result, breath returns to its most healthy state (Walker 2014). Diaphragmatic breathing cues or triggers the relaxation response. This benefits health by lowering heart rate, reducing oxygen demand, increasing relaxation, and improving core muscle stability.

During diaphragmatic breathing, a person consciously engages the diaphragm to take deeper breaths. As this happens, it is possible to notice the stomach rising and falling, or to feel an expanding or stretching sensation in the stomach rather than just in the chest.

Diaphragmatic Breathing

- Find a comfortable seated position with your feet on the floor. Check your posture to make sure that you have a clear airway.
- Place one hand on your chest and the other hand on the abdomen. Slow the thoughts and relax the mind.
- Begin breathing by drawing the breath down toward the stomach. You may feel the stomach push outward against the hand.
- Exhale and let the stomach fall inward.
- Continue this process without straining.
- Notice any changes in breath rate, length of inhalation versus exhalation, or chest versus belly movement.
- Add pleasant thoughts, images, or statements to go along with or enhance the experience.

Activity: Acupressure Routine: Smoothing Triple Warmer

Acupuncture, an ancient health technique, uses needles to stimulate important points on the body in order to promote natural self-healing. *Acupressure is a healing method that uses the hands rather than needles to work with many of the same body points.* Both acupuncture and acupressure focus on the meridians, energy systems that support specific organs and body systems. The meridians influence organs like the kidneys and liver, as well as systems like the digestive and nervous systems.

An important meridian system associated with the nervous system, is called Triple Warmer or Triple Burner. Triple Warmer is directly related to the stress response and includes several of the points (acupoints) associated with fight or flight (Feinstein 2005). This meridian system plays a critical role in regulation.

It is possible to work directly with Triple Warmer by using the hands to lightly trace points that calm or "smooth" nervous energy flow. The technique restores regulation and helps the body remember to cue the relaxation response.

Acupressure for Triple Warmer
From "Triple Warmer Smoothie" technique (Eden and Dahlin 2012)

- Rest your hands gently on your eyes and draw them over to your temples.
- Rest for several seconds.
- Slowly drag each hand above the ear, around the ear, down the neck, and to the shoulders.
- Rest for a several seconds.
- Gently squeeze each shoulder.
- Rest for several seconds.
- Slide your hands off your shoulders and cross them over your heart. Take five slow breaths.
- Rest for several seconds.
- Notice any feelings, images, thoughts, or changes.

Activity: Energy Portals

Meridian tapping techniques are becoming popular tools for addressing a variety of physical and mental health issues. These techniques use light finger taps to stimulate acupoints, the target points in the acupuncture system. Meridian tapping resets the body's electromagnetic systems and boosts natural energies. Scientists have recently developed technologies to observe the collections of points that influence specific organs and body processes (Church 2015).

Acupressure points are like energy buttons or portals that can be used to activate the body's self-healing. Tapping routines or protocols address physical health, psychological distress, wellness, and well-being (Feinstein 2022). There are several meridian points that are easy to locate and influence. These points increase regulation by helping the body calm and by balancing its energy systems.

The Karate Chop Point (KC)

One calming point is found on the hand near the little finger. The point is located on the side of the hand in the middle section or fleshy part between the top of the wrist and the base of the little finger. This area is sometimes called the karate chop point (KC) because a martial artist might use the side of the hand to deliver a blow to a board or opponent.

- Find the fleshy part or karate chop point on the side of the hand, below the pinky finger.
- Use two or three fingers from your other hand to lightly tap this area.
- Continue this process for one or two minutes.
- Remember to breathe.
- Check in and notice any changes in your stress or energy level.

Kidney Meridian (K 27)

The kidney meridian points support regulation, and the acupressure points K 27 (the twenty-seventh point on the kidney meridian) help reduce stress and anxiety. The K 27 points are located in the depressions below the collarbone, on both sides of the upper chest.

- Find K 27 by placing your fingertips on the spot where your collarbones meet. Place your fingertips about one quarter inch below the collarbone and move slightly outward. Feel for a small indentation.
- Tap lightly or rub this area with firm pressure.
- Notice any changes.

Try adding a soothing image, relaxing phrase, or positive self-statement while you tap.

CHAPTER 4

VERTICAL INTEGRATION: FEELING SAFE AND STAYING CALM

The vertical brain system is the one most often associated with dysregulation because it is home to the stress response. The vertical brain has three parts: the lower or "primitive" brain, the mid or emotional brain, and the cerebral cortex or upper brain. When these parts work together, information and energy smoothly flow in all directions, providing a foundation for responsive and effective problem-solving.

To help us survive, this flow is interrupted when the stress response is activated. While this change is essential during times of real threat, a disrupted brain state can become a default setting that derails the ability to respond to life's daily challenges in calm and thoughtful ways.

The Triad: Lower, Middle, and Upper Brain

The lower brain is located near the top of the neck and includes the brain stem. *The lower brain develops first and controls basic functions like breathing, blinking, and innate reactions like the startle response.*

The lower brain acts instinctually to make split-second decisions. It supports balance, movement, and motor processes that are essential to executive functioning. The lower brain is a foundation for performance skills that help us plan, organize, monitor, and manage complex tasks.

The mid or emotional brain lies deep within the brain itself, roughly behind the tip of the nose. *The mid brain contains the limbic system, a complex set of structures involved in emotion, motivation, learning, and memory.* This is the area that activates the stress response and is where strong emotions like anger and fear originate.

The mid brain's emotional center controls the release of the stress hormones cortisol and adrenalin, substances that stimulate the body's reactions to danger. The mid brain encloses the amygdala, an almond-shaped structure located deep within. The amygdala plays a significant role in monitoring danger and it has been referred to as the brain's smoke detector (Buczynski 2018).

The upper brain, or cerebral cortex, develops last, and is considered the most evolved area of the human brain. It is the seat of language, reasoning, imagining, and higher-order analytical thinking. *The upper brain is like a sophisticated command center that integrates the body and lower brain functions.* It is involved in complex activities like reflection, self-understanding, empathy, and morality.

Triad Brain

The upper brain: command center; higher level thinking and reasoning; self and other reflexive capacity

The mid brain: contains the limbic system; seat of emotions; initiates the stress response

The lower brain: controls basic functions; acts instinctually; supports executive functions

When the brain is integrated, higher-level thinking, mid-brain emotions, and lower functions work smoothly. During this top-down processing, the upper brain successfully handles challenging impulses and appropriately expresses the strong feelings that are generated in the mid brain. While this is happening, emotions enrich reasoning to help evaluate the benefits or merits of our actions and experiences. Simultaneously, the lower brain smoothly manages breathing and heart rate.

An integrated brain guides us toward actions and experiences that feel meaningful and have positive value, and away from those that are negative or destructive. We are able to remember a past mistake, calm a strong emotion, revise a decision, or form a new plan. The flow of energy and information is bi-directional: thoughts and feelings inform and update each other to serve our best interests with a sense of ease.

Under threat, vertical integration is disrupted and bottom-up processing takes place. Communication between the levels of the brain halts when the stress response activates, and the mid brain assumes control. The mid brain begins to exercise critical survival functions like sending chemical substances throughout the body. These substances prepare the body to fight, flee, freeze, or faint by increasing heart rate, elevating blood pressure, and boosting energy levels.

The disruption is highly adaptive in dangerous situations because it saves our lives. When the threat passes, the disconnection gradually subsides and the parts once again become integrated. We return to a state of bi-directional flow where our basic functions, feelings, and thoughts are once more integrated. However, when a child is chronically in bottom-up processing, this dysregulation pathway becomes firmly set in place.

Act Before Thinking or Think Before Acting?

The mid brain functions as a survival guide to ensure that we act before we think. This is an exquisite adaptation that puts us on high alert for mobilization and survival. Imagine hiking up a trail surrounded by tall grasses and suddenly hearing a noise. You see a bear and instantly your limbic system floods your body with the stress chemicals that prepare you for action.

You might fight, yelling, "Hey, bear," or retreat and back slowly away. Perhaps you freeze, hoping to become invisible. You do not take time to ponder the bear's size, shape, or color. You do not reminisce about bears you have seen in zoos or bear movies you enjoyed. You react in an instant to increase the likelihood of survival. *When the danger is real, like a bear or an oncoming car, it is best to act without thinking.*

With the chronic activation that results from toxic stress or trauma, the stress response system becomes overly sensitized and is easily triggered. *The stress response system can lose its effectiveness as our threat manager.* For example, on any given day there are situations that feel frustrating but that are not dangerous. Someone who honks at us in traffic may be inconsiderate or infuriating, but not life-threatening. Long shopping lines are inconvenient, but they do not merit rage or despair.

Under-Arousal

Vertical pathway dysregulation looks different in each individual. One child may yell or become defiant, while another looks sleepy, spacey, or tuned out. The latter presentations are consistent with under-arousal and freeze or faint.

Remember to consider that being under-aroused also signals dysregulation. When these children return to safety, help them raise their energy level by standing, moving, or engaging in a physical activity.

It is not helpful or healthy to be constantly keyed up because of a traffic jam, waiting in line, or a challenge at work. This may be what is happening when we see ourselves or someone else reacting badly in public or overreacting in general. Ongoing stress that does not subside impairs brain structures like the amygdala and the hippocampus (Van der Kolk 2015). Unfortunately, chronic activation of the stress response system has become commonplace.

Chronic stress has wide-reaching negative effects because it increases health risks. *When the stress response system is always active, its accompanying stress chemicals take a toll on the body by shutting down the immune system.* Cortisol in the short term improves learning and memory. In the long term, cortisol suppresses digestion and other resting functions, leading to immune-mediated disorders known as stress-related illnesses. Chronic stress also results in brain changes that decrease goal-directed behavior, impair memory, and cause problems with mood and sleep (Goleman 2008).

To meet the demands of a stressful modern world, it is important to learn how to return to top-down processing as quickly as possible, and to develop healthy vertical integration skills. While the stress response is critical for managing real threats, it becomes detrimental when it is established as a default setting. When the stress response process takes over in this way, we say we are "hijacked" by the emotional brain.

Hijacked: Ongoing Dysregulation

The stress response system activates whether a threat is real or not, terminating vertical integration. When activation is chronic, it creates a pathway for ongoing dysregulation and hijacking. The amygdala, a small, almond-shaped structure, plays a key role in this destructive pattern. The amygdala decides whether input from the senses signals the presence of danger. If so, it triggers the stress response. The amygdala bases its threat assessment on what is happening now as well as on all past experiences.

When past experiences include significant loss, injury, or trauma, the brain's appraisal system becomes distorted, creating an overactive sense of fear or anxiety. In this case, and even when the situation is safe, the amygdala links the current situation to a painful memory. It feels as if the past is happening in the present moment. Old traumas are evoked in the present moment and we experience feelings and sensations that may be unrelated to the current situation. We become hijacked.

Hijacking can cause us to act or overreact in unreasonable ways and it can be difficult to make sense of our feelings and behavior. Research has demonstrated that simply seeing pictures of angry or frightened faces can cause the amygdala to activate the stress response. The stress response can even be activated when the pictures are flashed below conscious awareness. The amygdala errs on the side of caution in order to protect us, but over time, it can become hypersensitive and overactive, triggering ongoing hijacking. As a result, we develop chronically defensive ways of engaging with the world.

Dangerous Dysregulation

Early toxic stress and amygdala damage have been implicated in chronic misperception of social situations and impulsive aggression (Hölzel et al. 2010).

Children with these tendencies often demonstrate serious disruptive behaviors that are dangerous and seemingly unrelated to the current situation. In these cases, threat assessment, safety planning, and contingency protocols should be created in advance to ensure everyone's safety.

Embodying Calm

We are designed to act without thinking during life-threatening situations, but in everyday moments we try to think before we act. The ability to stay integrated is a strong foundation for emotional and behavioral regulation. The faster we notice we are hijacked, the more quickly we can begin to downregulate.

Staying integrated is a complex process that requires a sophisticated set of skills. Given the speed and stealth with which the amygdala acts, as well as the powerful chemicals involved in fight or flight, integration is no small accomplishment. We need to notice and recognize personal triggers, the situations and experiences that prime us for hijacking.

While it is easy to know in retrospect what might have worked better in a given situation, it is challenging to choose to act differently in the moment. Calming the alarm circuitry requires overriding primitive survival mechanisms, managing our own stress responses, and exercising emotional competencies. As we develop these skills, we are better able to keep our cool when things get hot.

Main Ideas

When the vertical brain is integrated, thoughts, feelings, actions, and sensations are aligned and congruent, and there is a sense of being in tune with ourselves. We stay calm and responsive, and act in ways that are consistent with our best interests and values.

Once the stress response is triggered, acting without thinking optimizes survival. This becomes problematic when the safety appraisal system is overly-sensitized and the stressed state becomes a default setting. When this happens, we become reactive and defensive, misperceiving or distorting what is happening in the present moment. Language centers go offline and discussion only increases dysregulation.

It has become commonplace to experience negative stress, and there is solid evidence that chronic states of alertness lead to stress-related illnesses. These illnesses are the result of ongoing suppression of the immune system, as well as the suppression of the parasympathetic nervous system, which manages the digestive and resting functions.

It can be hard to know when we are being hijacked because some triggers occur below the level of our conscious awareness. Therefore, it is essential to be familiar with our internal states, and to have multiple strategies to help calm and downregulate in the moment.

Reader Reflection

Recall or review your understanding of the following and the role they play in vertical integration.

- Fight, flight, freeze, faint
- Triad brain
- Stress response
- Amygdala
- Hijacking
- Real versus perceived threat

Bring to mind the challenging person or situation from the previous reflections and consider these questions.

- Is someone easily triggered or chronically on high alert?
- How well do you stay integrated during stressful times?
- What strengthens your personal feelings of safety and calmness?
- What strategies do you employ to embody calm?

Think of a time you "freaked out," "flipped your lid," or "flew off the handle." Can you explain or make sense of your reaction differently now? Try the following questions.

- What do you usually say to yourself about what is going on when you become hijacked?
- What usually happens? Do you fight (argue), flee (fail to confront; seethe inwardly), or freeze/faint (shut down; abandon self or others)?
- When do you feel most unsafe and what are some of your biggest triggers?

Rehearse strategies that increase conscious awareness of triggers and patterns.

- Imagine the upper brain is being "taken over" by the limbic system. Suggest a strategy to yourself, such as breathing, pausing, or moving.
- Ask yourself or others for a "time out."

CHAPTER 5

VERTICAL ACTIVITIES AND EXPERIENCES: THE STRESS RESPONSE, MIND-BODY CONNECTION, AND EMOTIONAL INTELLIGENCE

The vertical brain works best when its three parts are integrated and serving an individual's best interests. We say that the vertical system becomes a regulation pathway as a way to indicate that it can function as a means for increasing or decreasing integration. The vertical system can become a pathway for dysregulation in challenging times like during hijacking or when the stress response is chronically activated. It is also a pathway for staying regulated when we use tools that keep us in top-down processing.

Vertical Integration Goals

Recognize: Children have default settings; I choose to respond rather than react.

Empathize: Toxic stress often plays a role in children's challenging behaviors.

Know: I can also be triggered and hijacked.

Resource: I help everyone feel safe and stay calm.

The exercises, activities, and resources presented in this chapter center on three main areas: managing the stress response, strengthening the mind-body connection, and increasing emotional intelligence. To maintain integration, it is essential to understand how the stress response operates to keep us safe, and then how it can become a default setting. It is critical to learn to maintain and model a calm demeanor while in the presence of a dysregulated child.

Some of the experiences are thought-based (cognitive-focused) and instructive, providing information about how the stress response system is activated and what escalation looks like.

These activities encourage readers to become more familiar with their own stress reactions, learn to identify personal triggers, and find ways to cue others in real time about their stress.

Several experiences are body-based (limbic-system focused) in order to illustrate and track the way escalation manifests in the body. There are activities meant to help children become aware of their own escalation processes in order to develop an ability to self-soothe during stressful encounters. Other experiences aim to increase emotional intelligence and to model ways to identify, work through, and master difficult emotions.

Each activity can be expanded or modified in any way to be most helpful and effective for the reader. See Chapter 3 for the movement, mindfulness, and energy exercises that might also be beneficial for this pathway.

Activity: Triad Brain

Daniel Siegel, M.D., is an internationally acclaimed author, award-winning educator, and renowned child psychiatrist. In his workshops, Dr. Siegel often illustrates the connection between the brain's emotional and reasoning parts by using a hand gesture. By changing the position of the fingers, the hand can represent stress response activation and show what happens when we are hijacked (Siegel and Bryson 2016).

Handy Brain Model

Reasoning brain: Fingers closed over in a fist

Emotional brain: Thumb hidden inside fist

Lower brain: Wrist and below

- Raise your hand—fingers straight, palm flat—as if you're asking a question. The wrist represents the lower brain or brain stem. This is the seat of automatic reactions such as breathing and balance.

- Next, curl your thumb in the center of the palm. The curled thumb represents the mid or emotional brain, the heart of the limbic system. It contains the amygdala and is the center of the stress response system.

- Now close your fingers around your thumb. The outer fingers correspond to the upper brain and higher level thinking. When the fist is closed, the brain is vertically integrated. The emotional brain nicely connects to the reasoning brain, and the lower brain supports the entire structure. Information and energy flow in both directions.

- When the brain detects a threat, the hand opens and the fingers are raised. This signifies the disconnection between the upper and mid brain. We have "flipped our lids." At this point, the emotional brain is sending chemical messages to override higher brain functions. Reasoning, language, and complex problem-solving skills become unavailable.

- Once the threat subsides, the stress chemicals are reabsorbed and the parts reconnect. We demonstrate this by once again covering the thumb with the fingers. The emotions calm, the thinking brain comes back online, and we are once again vertically integrated.

The model is a useful teaching tool that shows children what happens in the brain during the stress response. It is a real-time visual reminder that can be used as a silent reminder when someone begins to escalate. Once introduced, it can serve as a cue to downregulate or to access a calming resource like a quiet area or a breathing technique.

Activity: Stress Quadrant

The stress response is a powerful physiological process that impacts vertical integration and initiates fight, flight, freeze, or faint. We each have a potential for developing a "default setting," a chronic way of reacting to stress. This worksheet is a tool to increase awareness around how we and others handle stress.

- Create a quadrant chart and label each square with one of the four stress responses. Imagine or consider the thoughts, feelings, sensations, and actions that might accompany each reaction. Jot down descriptive words, images, memories, or other associations for each.

- Think back to a recent situation in which you felt stressed or threatened. What were your reactions? Which reaction is most typical for you? For example, do you usually argue, retreat, or go silent during a difficult situation?

Fight	Flight
Freeze	Faint

- Think of someone you know well. How does this person usually react when he or she is stressed? What are the person's most common signals?

- Consider what happens for you when someone else is reactive. Which of the four states is most triggering or difficult to handle?

Activity: Sense Maps

Although it is a common belief that humans have five senses used to see, hear, touch, taste, and smell, there is evidence that we have many more senses than previously imagined. *Interoception is a lesser-known sense that helps us feel and understand what is going on in our bodies.* Interoception tells us when we are hungry, full, hot, cold, or thirsty. We use it when we sense our heartbeat, pain level, and breathing.

By developing interoceptive skills, we are better able to anticipate the signals associated with the stress response. These internal sensations are like clues, hints that we are triggered and ready to flip our lids. We can use interoception like radar, as an early warning system that we are about to be hijacked. With practice, we can learn to predict what is coming and choose a strategy that helps us stay regulated and vertically integrated.

Use a graphics program, draw, or trace your body on butcher paper. Work independently or with a partner. Imagine a stressful situation or remember a difficult experience. Focus on this experience and notice your body sensations.

- What are the feelings? Where are any sensations located in your body?
- Do images, thoughts, or memories come up?
- What happens first? What feels biggest or most intense?

Locate and sketch, draw, or label the sensations, feelings, and images that make up your unique stress response signature. Examples might include drawing your face getting hot or your chest feeling tight. Others might be:

- Clenched fists;
- Seeing red; or
- Rushing sound in your ears.

Share your sense map with a partner. Describe what happens when you start getting stressed. Notice any similarities or differences between your maps. Brainstorm and share strategies that might help you stay calm.

Activity: In the Zone

When feelings and thoughts are connected, we are engaged and at our best. This state is sometimes referred to as being in the zone. The vertical brain is integrated as the head (upper brain), heart (mid brain), and base (lower brain) are congruent. Life is filled with purpose and pleasure.

In the zone, thoughts inform feelings, curb destructive impulses, and create appropriate responses. Meanwhile, feelings update thoughts, guide reasoning, and move us toward choices that serve happiness and higher interests.

Create a picture of what it is like when you are in the zone. Use an image, list, graph, collage, or favorite medium. Ask the following questions.

- What is it like in the zone?

- How do you get there? What keeps you there?

- When was the last time you were there?

- What drives you out of your zone? Examples might be lifestyle choices, other people, distractions, inner dialogue, or other factors.

Consider ways to limit disintegration and dysregulation.

- Name the biggest obstacles or challenges to staying in the zone.

- Brainstorm solutions. Create an action plan.

Activity: Pulse Biofeedback

Biofeedback is a set of mind-body techniques that use feedback to help someone recognize and influence physical signs of stress and anxiety. Biofeedback targets body awareness with the goal of strengthening the ability to influence the body's systems at will.

Increased heart rate is a common sign of stress that can be measured by taking the pulse directly or by using a heart rate monitor. These tools make it possible to notice how the heart rate changes throughout the day, and explore ways to directly influence the rate.

Heart rate and rhythm depend on whether a person is standing up or lying down, moving or staying still, feeling calm or feeling excited. A resting heart rate tends to be stable from day to day, and we usually connect good health with lower resting heart rates. In general, tension and stress alter the heart rate by elevating it.

Taking the Pulse

- To check your pulse at your wrist, place two fingers (usually the index and middle fingers) on the palm side of your other wrist, under the thumb and between the bone and the tendon. This is the location of the radial artery.

- When you feel your pulse, begin to count the number of beats during a 15-second interval. To calculate your beats per minute, multiply this number by four.

There is always a range of rates that are considered normal. For children ages six to fifteen, normal resting heart rates are between 70 and 100. For adults ages sixteen to sixty, normal rates range from 60 to 100.

Once you have mastered the technique, try exploring the relationship between your body and movement or between your body and your mind.

- Determine your resting heart rate, the usual rate when you are inactive. Check your pulse. Use a one-minute rhythm or movement technique. What do you notice?

- Check your pulse. Imagine, in detail, a stressful situation from the past. Check your pulse. Has there been a change? Check it again in five minutes. What do you notice?

- Determine your resting heart rate. Next, practice a three-minute mindfulness breathing technique. What do you notice?

- Remember the last time you were hijacked. What might have happened to your heart rate? Predict how this might change in the future.

Activity: Orienting for Overwhelm

Orienting is a technique that can help limit emotional overwhelm. The technique focuses on reentering the present moment by closely observing the environment. Orienting is a deliberate process meant to restore integration by reminding the brain that it is safe to be here now (Ogden and Fisher 2015). It is as if we are letting the amygdala know that someone is "in charge," appraising the situation and handling possible threat.

Orienting is similar to the game "I Spy," but it is played alone, in silence or aloud. It is most effective if a person begins to orient as soon as the person notices he or she is triggered.

Orienting Technique

- As soon as you are aware that you are becoming stressed, panicked, or overwhelmed, look around. Choose an object nearby and notice it in detail. Pay attention to characteristics and qualities like its size, shape, color, texture, depth. Name these aloud or describe them softly to yourself.

- Repeat this process for five objects. Focus on each object with intense concentration. Maintain attention and give a detailed descriptive commentary for each object. Take the time to really see and say what is in front of you.

How Does Orienting Work?

When we orient, we use perception, attention, language, and other skills to keep the upper brain engaged and to support vertical brain system integration.

Orienting returns a person to the present moment and helps reset the limbic system. This process consolidates the feeling of safety.

Activity: Body Scan

The body scan is a simple relaxation technique that is based on progressive muscle relaxation. It can calm the body and strengthen mind-body awareness. Muscle tension is one of the body's ways of responding to stress, and progressive relaxation techniques enhance deep muscle relaxation. Conscious, intentional relaxation can alleviate physical and emotional symptoms and distress.

A body scan focuses on internal sensations. The process builds interoceptive skills, the ability to recognize what is happening in the body, and helps us identify our unique stress signals. A body scan also helps us learn to cue the relaxation response. A body scan does not need to be long or complex and even three or four minutes is enough to produce increased relaxation. The following is an example of a script that can be easily adapted for any age level.

Four Minute Body Scan

- Sit comfortably with your feet on the floor. Your posture should support a good airway. Close your eyes or soften your gaze.
  - o Imagine leaving the activities of the day outside the door. Begin to draw your attention inward.
  - o (pause)
- Focus on your legs and feet. Notice any feelings or sensations.
  - o Whatever comes up for you is exactly right in this moment.
  - o (pause)
- Move your attention to your core. Notice your heart area or your stomach area.
  - o Stay on the surface or move inward
  - o Toward greater health and wellness.
  - o (pause)
- Bring your attention to your arms and hands.
  - o Check your shoulders or posture.
  - o Notice your elbows…wrists…fingers.
  - o (pause)

- Now move your attention to your neck and head.
  - ○ Check your jaw…is it loose or tight?
  - ○ Notice the back of your throat…is it open or closed?
  - ○ (pause)
- Notice your breath.
  - ○ Pay attention to the inhalation and the exhalation.
  - ○ Nothing else to do…just breathe.
  - ○ (pause)
- Now take four or five more breaths.
  - ○ Find yourself back here and now.
  - ○ (pause)
  - ○ Open your eyes.

Ask if anyone would like to share his or her experience. Emphasize that there is no right or wrong, and that whatever happened was just right for that moment. Treat all comments equally and with respect.

Activity: Cocoon

After a behavioral outburst, it is important for a child to recover his or her sense of safety, security, and self as quickly as possible. Downregulating begins a process that decreases the stress chemicals in the body, restores integration, and strengthens efficacy, a sense of mastery around self-management and control.

We often try to "think our way" out of distress and use the upper brain to soothe the upset. However, it is not possible to "talk ourselves" into being more regulated, especially while flooded with stress chemicals. Instead, it is more effective to use a somatic or body-based intervention that acts swiftly to shift the brain state (Ogden and Minton 2000). Body-based interventions target somatic regulation as way to reset the nervous system after a distressing event.

The Cocoon is a body-based self-soothing technique. It uses visualization and body posture to promote a sense of being wrapped in a protective container. The Cocoon technique can also incorporate bilateral stimulation, tapping on alternating sides of the body. Bilateral stimulation is a technique used in the treatment of trauma-related disorders (Shapiro 2017).

To create a cocoon, a child imagines himself or herself wrapped in a comforting covering. The child may then lightly tap on alternating sides of the arms.

Cocoon Script

- Imagine yourself inside a protective covering. You are comfortable, safe, and everything is just right. This is your cocoon. It may be like a warm blanket, a colorful quilt, or a magical wrap.

- Cross your arms and wrap them around the front of your body in a cozy and relaxing way. Let your hands rest on the outside of your arms.

- Notice your cocoon.
  - o Is it large or small?
  - o What color is it?
  - o What does it feel like?
  - o What makes it special?

- Tap your fingers lightly on one arm and then tap on the other arm. Repeat. You can tap slowly or quickly; you choose. Continue for two or three minutes or as long as it feels comfortable.

- Notice how you feel now. Remember, you can take your cocoon with you wherever you go and use it whenever you want to relax and feel safe.

Activity: Savoring

To savor is to focus intentionally on a positive event or experience while engaging all of the senses to heighten pleasurable thoughts, feelings, sensations, and images. Savoring is a process that anchors a positive brain state in the body. We use deliberate and elaborate thinking and language to amplify the relaxed feeling state that reduces stress and generates a sense of well-being (Seligman 2006).

Just as we savor a delicious food, we can learn to savor dozens of daily experiences. The experience does not need to be an extraordinary feat or triumph. Instead, it is possible to savor a simple thing like how it feels to pet a favorite animal, feel sunshine, rest your eyes, or sit in a comfortable chair. Linger on positive details that cue the body toward relaxation, heighten contentment, and halt the treadmill of never-ending expectation and activity.

Savoring also strengthens the memory. Like so many brain functions, memory becomes stronger with sustained attention and use. Bookmarking positive experiences helps children relax, self-soothe, and build resilience. As a child learns to re-experience a positive event, the child extends ways to manage his or her feelings.

- Plan regular opportunities for savoring with students, friends, colleagues, and others. Engage all of the senses to enhance the experience.

- Practice savoring regularly. Notice any changes in stress level, connection, or well-being. If helpful, use a rating scale to help track change.

Activity: Visual Analogy

Although behavioral outbursts may seem to come out of the blue, they usually build over time. Highly-attuned adults notice their build-up signals, like a side glance, angry expression, or rigid posture. These adults use attuned perception to predict and intervene before a blowup or meltdown happens. Children can also learn to notice their signals with the support of a visual analogy. A visual analogy is an interactive tool that helps children track their escalation processes.

Visual analogies use pictures or objects to represent the feelings, thoughts, sensations, events, and interactions that occur as a child becomes dysregulated (Kenney and Young 2015). Introduce the project when a child is regulated and shows a high level of willingness to engage. It is important for the process to feel collaborative rather than threatening or punitive. This decreases the likelihood of triggering and offers an opportunity to be curious without moving into defensiveness or emotional overwhelm.

Building a Visual Analogy

- Have the child select a picture from a magazine or generate a computer image that captures a difficult feeling, thought pattern, or behavior. Common themes are anger, aggression, loneliness, worry, fear, or disappointment. The images might show a stormy sea, tornado, monster, or steep mountain.

- Create a title. An example might be "Mountain of Fear," a jagged peak for a dangerous, solitary trek. Another example is "The Chaos Tornado," an out-of-control whirlwind that destroys all in its path.

- Have the child "look around" the image, for significant or remarkable features or landmarks. Pay attention to any that correspond to what happens during the emotional or behavioral escalation process. Ask questions like the following.

- How do you know when you are heading up the mountain or when the tornado is coming?
- What happens inside you or around you?
- What do you see, feel, taste, or touch as you move upward?
- What happens next?
- Is anyone with you?
- Can you stop going forward? Can you turn it around?
- What is it like at the top?
- How do you get down?

- Help the child track the journey from both an internal and external perspective, noticing what happens inside and what happens in the environment. Increase self-awareness by using "I" statements and by noticing internal dialogue (what we say to ourselves).

- Notice relevant bodily sensations. Identify environmental triggers.

- Show support and acceptance during the discussion. Help the child maintain a sense of safety and distance as the child notices, describes, and tracks the trajectory. Use downregulation techniques and check in frequently, monitoring the level of distress.

The visual analogy can be used in real time during escalation as a visual cue or a subtle reminder to notice what is going on in the moment. After a negative incident and when all parties are once again regulated, it can be used as a debriefing tool.

Activity: The Weather Within

The weather is everywhere and we can use its universal language to express our moods and feelings. Some days are warm and others are rainy. We too can feel warm and sunny, or stormy and blue. Feelings, thoughts, sensations, and inner experiences tell us whether we are bright, cloudy, or frozen, and can let us know when a storm is coming.

Children can use weather terms to express what might otherwise feel overwhelming or unsafe. A child's inner weather might be dark or light, pleasant or unpleasant, calm or unpredictable. The child's feelings become clouds that grow and spread, shift, or move out of sight.

Have children create a personal weather report using language from the wind, clouds, rain, and so on. Use questions to deepen the process.

- What is the weather like inside you today?
- When is it sunny? How do you know?
- What is your favorite weather?
- What changes the weather for better or worse?

A weather report can predict changing conditions. Track "weather patterns" using a graph or other visual tool.

- Is the wind picking up or is a storm passing?
- Which direction is the temperature going?

Forecasting: It is important to learn to handle bad weather. Although no one "controls" the weather, there are good ways to manage and respond. For example, when a tornado is coming, a warning siren signals potential danger. This helps everyone prepare and stay safe.

Use forecasting to help children access resources and move to pre-arranged safety planning.

- How can you let others know about an upcoming storm?
- Is there a way to put up an umbrella?
- Where could you take shelter or relocate?

Activity: Online Resources

Regulation, the stress response, and neuroplasticity are becoming popular topics for educators, counselors, and parents. Below are a few of the many excellent online resources that target regulation and brain-training skills.

https://developingchild.harvard.edu/

The Harvard Center on the Developing Child is an excellent resource for parents and educators. The Center describes itself as a multidisciplinary team committed to science-based innovation. It maintains that advances in science should be used to support a promising future for every child.

The site provides articles and videos on important child-related topics, like brain and body health and child development. Several excellent videos explore the negative effects of toxic stress on growth and learning. The site also includes parenting articles that promote healthy regulation.

https://www.jensenlearning.com/

Eric Jensen, Ph.D., is an author and former teacher devoted to brain-based learning. He has been synthesizing research and developing practical applications for educators since the 1990s. Dr. Jensen blends cutting-edge brain-based science with school-based teaching strategies.

Two of Dr. Jensen's best-known works are *Teaching with the Brain in Mind* and *Tools for Engagement: Managing Emotional States for Learner Success.* He has written more than twenty-eight books on topics aimed at enhancing learning and behavior in the classroom setting.

https://drdansiegel.com/

Dan Siegel, M.D., is an internationally recognized authority on child development, attachment, parenting, mindfulness, and interpersonal neurobiology. He has published extensively for both professional and non-professional readers and many of his works are referenced in this book.

Dr. Siegel is also a well-known presenter. His website offers an online learning program. He has published several informative books for parents including *The Whole-Brain Child, No-Drama Discipline,* and *The Yes Brain.*

Explore the sites listed above or investigate others. Create a list of resources to share with colleagues or interested friends. Create a library in your school or workplace.

Activity: Emotional Intelligence (EQ)

Emotional intelligence encompasses proficiencies like being able to recognize, know about, cope with, express, and manage feelings in ourselves and others (Eckman 2003). Identifying and talking about emotions can transform our relationships. A good emotional vocabulary lets us express our needs and ask for support from others.

There are also beneficial effects on emotional overwhelm. Naming feelings calms down the emotional circuitry in the brain while activating language centers helps dampen an overactive amygdala. Labeling emotions is related to better emotional regulation and psychosocial well-being. When we can talk about our feelings, we are better at managing the ups and downs of ordinary existence.

Higher Emotional Intelligence

Increased ability to recognize how others feel and show empathy
Better at regulating moods and emotions
Greater ability to solve problems and get needs met
Easier to influence others

Lower Emotional Intelligence

Less able to accept feedback, even if constructive
Decreased conflict resolution
Increased mental health symptoms, especially anxiety and depression
Poorer relationship outcomes

While working with feelings is challenging for adults, it can be even more difficult for children. Young people are only beginning to associate body sensations and signals with feeling states. They may also avoid "big" feelings like anger and sadness because they feel threatening, unacceptable, or shameful. Fortunately, there are many wonderful feeling charts and graphics that can help people of all ages learn to identify and talk about feelings. The charts show an almost endless variety of emotions.

Choose an age-appropriate feeling chart, computer graphic, or set of emojis. Try some of the following prompts.

- Point to a feeling that you have had. What do you call this feeling? What was happening when you felt this? What else might go on to make someone feel this?

- Point to a feeling that you like best. Why do you like it? What happens in your body when you feel this? What might be happening in the situation?

- Point to a feeling that you dislike or that feels uncomfortable. Where do you feel this in your body? What do you do when you have this feeling?

Expand the discussion and identify the thoughts, sensations, and actions that usually accompany a feeling.

- Talk about the differences between having a feeling and acting out a feeling.

- Brainstorm good ways to handle tough feelings. Strategies might include positive ways to express, contain, move beyond, or share feelings with others. Draw from present experiences or examples from books, movies, etc.

Model strong emotional intelligence. Talk about your own feelings and share strategies and successes.

CHAPTER 6

SPECIALIZATION AND THE HORIZONTAL BRAIN

The brain is usually pictured showing its two signature parts, the hemispheres. The hemispheres lie side by side and make up most of the brain's size. Each hemisphere specializes in particular tasks and processes, and this specialization is called lateralization. Lateralization helps account for the endless diversity we find in human beings.

Hemisphere development influences how we think and feel, our cognitive and affective styles, and how we perceive and process information. An individual's hemisphere profile reflects unique skills, abilities, preferences, and perspectives. These individual differences make us successful builders, musicians, or nurses, and may explain why we enjoy different activities, such as reading novels, solving puzzles, or dancing.

When we accept personal differences, we validate others and model tolerance and inclusion. When a child is validated, he or she relaxes and feels seen, appreciated, and understood. This felt sense helps the child stay regulated as he or she engages in the world. When children are criticized or excluded for thinking, feeling, or being different, they shut down or act out, and may fail to actualize and meet their highest potential.

Early Development and the Hemispheres

The right brain is the dominant hemisphere for most of childhood. The right side is associated with nonverbal language and it has been referred to as the survival brain. The right hemisphere utilizes emotional and sensory memory (Siegel 1999). The left brain is associated with verbal and analytic abilities. The left brain develops slower than the right and matures after about age eighteen. It has growth spurts around the time language develops and also during adolescence.

The brain hemispheres communicate by sending information across the corpus callosum, a broad band of nerve fibers that joins the two sides. This strip develops slowly, and becomes fully mature at around the age of twelve. Healthy development of the corpus callosum is required for efficient left-right brain communication. Strong left-right brain communication increases the capacity to take in diverse types of information and employ different kinds of thinking. Effective communication between the hemispheres also makes it easier to rewire and make lasting changes in the brain.

Hemisphere development can be stalled by negative early experiences. Just as toxic stress affects stress response settings, early developmental threats, such as chronic infection, exposure to environmental toxins, poor nutrition, ongoing stress, and lack of educational stimulation can have neurobehavioral consequences (Stein and Kendall 2014). These early life factors affect cognitive processes and social learning, impacting intellect and aptitude.

Poor hemisphere communication and hemisphere weaknesses lead to limited ways of engaging with others and with the world (Jensen 2017). Hemisphere deficits become pathways for the regulation and behavioral challenges observed in difficult children. It is important to provide experiences aimed at strengthening weaknesses and developing compensatory skills, optimizing balance and complementarity.

Specialization: Taking Sides

The hemispheres operate as a pair, although they may show marked differences in levels of development and complexity. One hemisphere may appear to dominate, but no side works independently on its own. When we describe someone as right-brained or left-brained, we are likely referring to distinct or prominent ways a person thinks, acts, or comes across to others.

The right hemisphere is often described as holistic. *The right brain processes images, recognizes and generates patterns, and sees the whole picture.* The right brain is in charge of assigning meaning to an experience, and creates a "felt-sense" for situations and events. The right hemisphere uses non-verbal language to interpret facial expressions, tone of voice, posture, gestures, and eye contact.

The right hemisphere modality is influenced by information coming from the body, including the "gut" and the lower brain areas. When people describe themselves as right-brained, they likely see themselves as highly sensitive, artistic, imaginative, and possessing a high emotional intelligence.

The left hemisphere is where word processing, linear thinking, detail recognition, and fine motor action happen. *The left brain best employs reason, analysis, and cause-and-effect models.* Left-brained thinkers might be characterized as logical and literal, and may enjoy mathematics, problem-solving, and creating "inside the box." When people describe themselves as left-brained, they may see themselves as more rational, place less emphasis on feelings, and be more likely to use linear problem-solving methods.

The left brain is most comfortable dealing within areas that are already bounded or known, while the right hemisphere is associated with the realm of the unknown. Each side is invaluable in managing even the simplest task.

Healthy, balanced development is associated with comprehensive and efficient problem-solving and a keen ability to manage challenges. When the hemispheres work together, they are like a computer running many simultaneous and complementary subroutines and programs. When we develop both sides of our brains, we become "whole-brained," unlocking the resources and abilities to successfully meet life's demands (Siegel and Bryson 2011).

Hemisphere Dominance

Neither hemisphere works alone, and no one is solely right-brained or left-brained. However, strong interests and skills may reflect a "dominant" side.

Hemisphere dominance influences our levels of comfort with open-ended questions and is associated with the ability to manage risk (Peterson 1999).

Hemisphere differences also influence how we respond to different kinds of information and even whether we identify as a liberal or a conservative (Schreiber et. al. 2013).

Diversity and Inclusion

Hemisphere strengths and weaknesses affect the kind of information we take in, and how much we value that type of information. Specialization accounts for diversity in areas like communication, social ability, logic, literacy, and visual-spatial skills. It affects areas like creativity, nature awareness, dexterity, musical ability, and spiritual strengths (Armstrong et. al. 2012).

Specialization shows its dark side when deficits or imbalances distort how we perceive and act in the world. Distortions can lead to biases in information processing and problem-solving. When this happens, there is a tendency to be rigid or judgmental, accompanied by a disinclination to entertain alternative perspectives. It seems natural to devalue or exclude those who are different. The horizontal brain becomes a pathway for dysregulation for self and others.

When we own our personal strengths or weaknesses, we are more likely to consider their impact on others. Someone who values creativity may have an active and unstructured office or classroom. Some children will thrive in this environment. Others who operate best with structure and routine may have difficulty navigating this environment and become anxious and dysregulated. The point is not that one approach is better than another, but that when we understand the implications of differences, we may successfully accommodate them.

Two Operating Systems

One way to think about specialization is to imagine that our brains contain two operating systems. The right hemisphere initiates exploration when the terrain is unfamiliar and we do not know what to do. The left side assumes command once we are secure.

Children with challenging behaviors often show strong hemisphere preferences that lead them to disregard or distrust messages coming in through unfamiliar channels. Adults who acknowledge and accommodate for this can increase learning and improve communication.

When we address skill deficits and develop complementary proficiencies, we strengthen the capacity to regulate. By expanding or strengthening lesser developed hemisphere skills, we create a more balanced hemisphere profile. With complementarity, we focus on strengthening ways that one hemisphere might support, compensate for, or enhance the other side. Interventions draw on existing skills, and use them to scaffold weaker areas.

Skilled adults who work with neurodiverse populations take differences into account and meet children in respectful and inclusive ways. Children who feel appreciated, in spite of their unique thinking and feeling styles, learn to manage themselves actively and have fewer meltdowns or shutdowns. When we celebrate differences and help others feel seen and valued, they are more likely to stay regulated.

Main Ideas

Hemisphere specialization is an ongoing brain process where each side of the brain develops in complexity. Every person has a unique hemisphere "profile" that reflects individual skills, abilities, interests, and attitudes, as well as preferred ways to receive information and solve problems. Specialized or dominant ways of being and seeing the world can become the basis for rigid judgement and bias.

The right brain develops first and is primarily non-verbal. The right brain is feeling-centered, meaning-making, and explorative. The left brain is more dominant beginning in adolescence. It uses the verbal and narrative memory, and acts like a chief executive in charge of planning and problem-solving.

When toxic stress, environmental exposures, and negative health events derail healthy hemisphere development, children miss out on acquiring foundational skills. Poor communication between the hemispheres also interferes with the potential for success.

We feel seen and appreciated when others tolerate our differences, value our perspective even when they do not agree, and treat us with respect regardless of difference in rank or ability. Feeling accepted and appreciated in spite of differences is a requirement for learning and healthy engagement, and helps us to stay regulated.

Reader Reflection

Specialization is our brain's elegant way of approaching and solving complicated problems. It is like drawing on two complementary operating systems. While the theory of "dominance" has been debunked, lateralization, the division of functions between the two hemispheres, is widely accepted.

Although no one has one side that works independently on its own, each of us shows preferences for right- or left-brain processes and thinking. Consider the following questions.

- With which hemisphere do you typically identify? Do you consider yourself right-brained, left-brained, or balanced? How do you know?
- What is one strength of your hemisphere style?
- Describe how right- or left-brained preferences or deficits impact learning and behavior.
- How does your classroom, office environment, or program accommodate diversity?
- How does your hemisphere style impact your communication or instruction?
- How can you incorporate more balance and complementarity in your curriculum or program?

Consider the child or situation you identified in the earlier reflections or choose another problematic situation.

- Are hemisphere deficits or differences factors in the situation?
- Are there diversity or inclusion areas to consider?

Brain lateralization helps us negotiate multi-step problems and engage in complex tasks, but strong biases can lead to rigidity and decrease the ability to solve problems.

- Can you recognize a strong dominance or bias in yourself or anyone else you know?
- Create an action plan.

CHAPTER 7

HORIZONTAL ACTIVITIES AND EXPERIENCES: AWARENESS, COMPLEMENT AND BALANCE, AND BRAIN-BASED WELLNESS

Hemisphere development affects our talent for thinking, feeling, and expressing ourselves; influences the kind of information we can access and are comfortable with; and shapes which methods we use to solve problems. Hemisphere skills either further or limit the ability to pay attention, engage, learn, and feel competent. The horizontal pathway can be impeded due to developmental factors or when we are rejected or criticized for our differences. We are then likely to shut down or act out. When validated by others, we stay relaxed and regulated.

Horizontal Goals

Recognize: Each hemisphere profile is unique; I choose to consider this rather than criticize.

Empathize: Toxic stress often plays a role in neurodevelopmental deficits and differences.

Know: My own weaknesses and biases influence how I perceive others and the world.

Resource: I help everyone feel seen, validated, and included.

The resources, exercises, and activities presented in this chapter center around the areas of hemisphere awareness, balance and complementarity, and brain-based wellness. Some activities are psychoeducational, such as comparing the two hemispheres or strengthening related skills for balance and complementarity. A few exercises focus on noticing how people engage in and navigate the world in distinct ways.

Some activities aim to raise awareness about dominance patterns and how these influence attitudes and behavior. Uncovering personal preference patterns opens opportunities to move away from biases and toward greater acceptance and inclusion. The last exercises introduce wellness tools and technologies that directly influence the brain.

All of the activities can be expanded or modified in any way to be most helpful and effective for the reader. See Chapter 3 for the movement, mindfulness, and energy exercises that would also be beneficial for this pathway.

Activity: Hemisphere Awareness

Are you "right-brained" or "left-brained?" Although these are informal terms, they hint at individual personality or problem-solving style. For example, we might refer to a logical, linear thinker with an attention to detail as left-brained. Someone who comfortably communicates feelings and who gets the big picture might be described as right-brained.

Hemisphere Attributes:

Left	Right
– Logic emphasis	– Feeling emphasis
– Detail-oriented	– Big-picture oriented
– Words and language	– Symbols and images
– Math and science	– Spatial perception
– Order and pattern	– Meaning-making
– Reality focused	– Imagination focused
– Forms strategies	– Generates possibilities
– Practical and safe	– Risks the unknown

- Notice any quality that you strongly identify with. Give an example of how this influences your relationships or activities.

- Is there an attribute that you see as a weakness? Where does it come up in your work, life, or relationships?

- Which qualities do you value most? Are there attributes that you resist or dislike? Give examples from your day-to-day experience.

- Which quality would you like to develop? Create an action plan.

- Consult with a trusted friend or colleague and share ideas and goals for building more balance or complementarity.

Assessing Cognitive, Personality, and Learning Styles

Assessment tools can help the individual better understand how he or she thinks, learns, and performs, and there are many popular tools available in educational or professional settings.

Some questionnaires focus on decision-making or learning styles, and others measure how we perceive, process, and order information. These tools increase self-awareness and can provide insight about hidden assumptions and biases.

Activity: Mapping Sides

Having a unique hemisphere profile means that each of us can do some things well but will need help with others. It is important to explore these ideas with care and in a manner that does not demean or threaten those who may feel vulnerable.

I.

Create a hemisphere map and list, describe, or illustrate the two hemispheres and the skills and qualities associated with each.

- Draw the brain hemispheres using a medium such as butcher paper, poster board, or a computer graphics program. Compile or find an age-appropriate list of the qualities, characteristics, skills, subjects, and processes commonly associated with each side.

- Have participants label each side and list or draw its attributes.

Consider the following questions.

- What are you good at? How do you know?

- What is hard for you to do? How do you get help?

- What do you wish you could do or be better at?

Have the students share their answers in pairs or groups. Introduce age-appropriate terms like balance, complementarity, bias, neurodiversity, and so on.

II.

Lead a guided discussion focusing on hemisphere specialization with your colleagues or students. Invite participants to share their experiences or concerns about dealing with those who are different. Use the discussion to raise awareness around issues of diversity and inclusion.

Activity: Cooperating Hemispheres

Each brain hemisphere is dedicated to particular skills or processes, but both sides contribute and work together to complete even simple tasks. For example, counting to three or walking in a straight line requires the cooperation of both hemispheres.

To get a sense of how hemispheres work together, select a short task. Examples might be singing a song, cooking a meal, or drawing a picture. Break the activity into small parts and create a sequence of events. Label the hemisphere that is most likely involved in each part of the task.

Example: Cooking a meal

Choose a recipe

- Left brain: forms a strategy, processes words and language
- Right brain: generates possibilities, risks the unknown, imagines the outcome

Open cupboard to gather ingredients

- Right brain: uses spatial perception, gross motor movement
- Left brain: uses fine motor skills, realistic appraisal, pays attention to details

Begin measuring

- Right brain: spatial perception, gross motor movement
- Left brain: mathematics, attention to detail, fine motor skills

Notice how each discrete skill requires both left and right brain functions. Which skills seem easy and which seem more difficult? Have participants share their ideas with a partner or in a small group.

Activity: Dominance and Stereotypes

Although hemisphere dominance tests are not considered valid scientific assessments, they can be fun and informal ways to explore personal preferences and styles. Many of these tools are found on the internet by googling "hemisphere dominance test." Before taking an online test, have students review the skills and qualities associated with each hemisphere.

Prior to testing

- Work in pairs or groups. Have students predict their dominant sides.

- Share predictions and give examples. If they are comfortable, have students ask for feedback about their predictions.

Online hemisphere dominance test

- Have the students complete an age-appropriate online hemisphere cognitive-style test. Discuss the results with a partner or in a small group. Compare the findings to earlier predictions.

- Identify hemisphere goals like acquiring a valuable skill or developing an area of interest. Examples might be wanting to be better at math or learning to play an instrument. Develop an action plan.

During the discussion, ask if any uncomfortable or uncomplimentary language or labels came up. These might be slang terms used to describe differences that are seen as unpopular or unattractive.

- Discuss how labels can reflect biases or stereotyping. Explore how individual bias influences the way that we see another person's strength and weakness.

- Ask about personal experiences with being stereotyped, labeled, or put down. Brainstorm solutions focused on respecting individual difference and diversity.

- Discuss why acceptance, appreciation, and tolerance are important.

Activity: Whole Brain Storytelling

The stories we tell ourselves shape us. What we say inside can inspire and motivate, or reinforce our confusion and helplessness. By using informed conversation techniques, we can help children stay regulated as they talk about difficult experiences. Questions and comments that draw from both hemispheres balance perspective and strengthen self-worth.

Caring listeners who use both right- and left-brain questions assist integration, help generalize learning, and increase self-mastery (Mendoza and Bradley 2021). A left-brain strategy, like asking for facts or recalling details, can create a container for painful feelings and limit their ability to overwhelm. What is frightening or unmanageable becomes easier to hold. When a narrative seems rote or lacks emotion, right-brain strategies like imagining, using toys or manipulatives, or drawing a picture can enrich understanding.

When questions or comments engage both hemispheres, they scaffold the child's narrative and increase his or her sense of coherent meaning. Intentionally crafted conversations can draw out an introvert, soothe the anxious, or calm an angry child (Siegel and Bryson 2011). Whole-brain stories promote self-understanding, self-mastery, and reconsolidation. Reconsolidation is a process in which individuals find healthy ways to respond to difficult experiences.

Below are some hemisphere-related questions and comments to create a whole brain narrative experience.

Left-Brain Qualities

- Ask for or provide the facts (who, what, where, when, why, how).
- Create a detailed sequence of events.
- Use rich, descriptive language.
- Ask problem-solving questions.

Right-Brain Qualities

- Ask for or name the feelings involved.
- Represent what happened using figures, symbols, or images.
- Draw a picture or "map" of an important event.
- Imagine a different or better ending.
- Tell the story as if it were a dream.

Activity: Crossing the Midline

Educational kinesiology programs like Brain Gym or Bal-A-Vis aim to increase brain and body integration through movement patterns. The patterns are designed to enhance brain activity and connectivity in ways that benefit learning, health, and resilience. In many of these activities, the goal is to increase the information and energy crossing the corpus callosum. Crossover motor rhythms establish a framework for pattern sequencing and prepare the brain for higher-order thinking (Hubert 2014).

Crossover movement patterns, actions that cross the midline of the body, are particularly popular. Movement on the right side of the body is tracked by the left brain, and movement on the left is tracked by the right brain. When we move our hands across the midline in front of our body, we activate both hemispheres.

Find or create age-appropriate movement patterns that include crossovers. The figure eight is a common pattern for crossing the midline. The figure eight pattern can be subtle or part of a larger movement routine. Below are some examples.

- Draw as many figure eights in the air as you can using small and large figures.

- Move to music and surround yourself with figure eights.

- In pairs and without touching, draw figure eight patterns around your partner.

- Face a partner and slowly create a pattern or sequence of moves that crosses the midline. Have your partner mirror each movement. Change roles.

Activity: Brain-Based Wellness

In a fast-paced world, we are surrounded by high levels of stress. Whether the stress is physical, emotional, or environmental, it affects brain health, leading to damage and disease. Brain-based wellness is a growing healthcare area that offers tools and technologies to counter the negative effects of stress and to help us cope and flourish. Brain-based wellness is a broad field targeting diverse goals like calming the over-stimulated nervous system, increasing hemisphere balance, and working with brainwave states and flow.

Wellness tools target processes like biofeedback, synchronization, coherence, and state change. Many wellness tools are available to the general public while others are administered by licensed professionals. The tools introduced below are just a few that are currently available, and are intended to familiarize the reader with this growing field.

Neurofeedback is a type of biofeedback that helps an individual learn how to change his or her brain's physiological activity in order to improve health and performance. Neurofeedback activates areas in the brain that support changes in thinking, mood, and behavior. Several simple programs are available for home use, and other programs require a skilled professional (Soutar and Longo 2011).

QEEG is a type of neurofeedback that is administered in an office setting by a medical or clinical professional. QEEG (quantitative electroencephalography) or EEG (electroencephalography) biofeedback use precise instruments, electrodes, and sophisticated computer programs to measure the brain's electrical activity and provide feedback to the user.

Neural entrainment is the basis for popular wellness products. Entrainment theory proposes that the brain operates best when its frequencies are aligned. Alignment is optimized by using external rhythms, like music beats, to synchronize brainwave frequencies. These rhythms help the brain move into optimal states, and target stress relief, increased attention, and improved sleep.

Transcranial magnetic stimulation or TMS delivers a magnetic pulse to stimulate nerve cells in specific regions of the brain. TMS is delivered in a doctor's office via an electric coil placed on the head. In order to improve mood, for example, the coil is used to activate areas in the brain that show decreased activity. TMS is used primarily for the relief of depression and other mood-related disorders.

Heart rate variability or HRV measures the variation in time between each heartbeat. Variation in heart rates is controlled by the autonomic nervous system (ANS), which regulates our heart rate, blood pressure, breathing, and digestion. When we are in an anxious state, the variation between subsequent heartbeats is low and when we are in a more relaxed state, the variation between beats is high. Easy-to-use and inexpensive HRV tools include phone apps, the EmWave2, and personal heart rate monitors.

CHAPTER 8

SOCIAL ENGAGEMENT AND
THE CONNECTED BRAIN

The brain is a social organ that uses interactions and relationships to learn about itself, others, and the world. Connecting with others is a deep-seated human need, and moving toward others for contact, support, and care is hard-wired in the human brain. We are born helpless, and our survival depends on being nurtured by our caregivers. The ability to form positive relationships enhances regulation and resilience, and is an important part of the social engagement system.

The social engagement system uses information derived from what people do, as well as from their body language, voice quality, and facial expressions. Social engagement relies on mirror neurons, a specialized class of brain cells that help us interpret and understand the actions of others. The mirror neuron network lays a foundation for emotion, communication, and self-regulation (Schore 2015).

The Mirror Neuron System

When we see someone perform an action, motor neurons activate or fire in response, mirroring the other person. Our brains act as if we were also performing the action. When we observe someone eating, our own electrical patterns associated with eating also fire. When we watch someone grasp a pencil, our brains activate reciprocal motor neurons. *Mirror neurons allow us to grasp what another person is doing and what he or she has in mind.*

The mirror system plays an important role in social development. It shapes how we respond by teaching us to make sense of how others act.

The system helps us learn to identify our internal states and experiences, and to sort out our beliefs, intentions, and desires. We then attribute these to another person and are able to interpret, explain, and predict behavior.

Growing evidence suggests mirror neurons are the cornerstone of human empathy. When we observe someone get hurt, we ourselves can feel uncomfortable sensations or pain, and may even say, "Ouch." This is more than just thinking about another's pain. Instead, neurons in our own brains are reproducing the experience. This process becomes a basis for empathic attunement and compassion.

Social Engagement as Resource

The social engagement system has several important functions. First, it moves us toward caregivers. As we connect with those who assist, support, and sustain us, we optimize our survival. Caregivers, allies, and advocates help us manage life's challenges and are some of our greatest resources. Each positive relationship strengthens self-esteem and efficacy, the sense that we can be effective in the world. Healthy connection protects us from depression, anxiety, and the threats that result from isolation (Center on the Developing Child 2011).

Healthy engagement strategies also mitigate developmental damage by offering the opportunity to experience connections that bring help and that feel good. Positive social engagement fosters security and worth, builds resilience, decreases stress reactivity, and strengthens the capacity to form enduring relationships.

A healthy engagement system is fundamental to regulating emotions and behavior. When others listen and are there for us, we recover quickly from threat or stress and it is easier to downregulate (Siegel 2007). After debriefing with a friend or significant other, we easily regain equilibrium. Life does feel better with a little help from our friends.

Contagious Emotions: When My Dysregulation Becomes Your Dysregulation

Early trauma disrupts the developing brain's social engagement structures. *Without direct intervention, children with histories of toxic stress may never establish secure foundations for affiliation and belonging.* For these children, adults are not sources of support or regulation, and instead are experienced as harmful or dangerous. When this is the case, young people fail to reach out, even to nurturing adults.

Destructive past relationships can create significant distortion in how we perceive and relate to others. When relationships have failed to offer necessary support, children develop heightened tendencies toward dysregulation. This is another example of neuroplasticity's dark side that makes it hard to tell friend from foe or to reach out to others in healthy ways. These children are also overly sensitive to dysregulation in the environment and are prone to mirroring or taking on the dysregulated states of others.

Models of entrainment and emotional contagion help illustrate this point. Entrainment is a process where the movement or frequency of one physical or biological system activates, changes, or entrains the motion or frequency of another system. Entrainment in human beings happens via mirror neurons when one person's brainwave state synchronizes or changes the brainwave state of another person. Through entrainment, it is possible to "pass on" an emotional state.

This can also be referred to as emotional contagion, because it is similar to what happens in a disease model. Just as it is possible to pick up or pass on germs to one another through close contact, brain wave states can also be passed on or entrained. You may have experienced something like this when you were uplifted by someone's joy or when you "picked up" someone's bad mood in spite of your best efforts not to do so.

The good news is that even when we come into contact with a negative state, if we are able to avoid reflecting it back into the situation, we create a corrective experience. *Corrective experiences help children grow beyond what they have known.* When we use healthy social strategies, in spite of negative emotional contagion, we refrain from reinforcing distorted patterns of engagement (Siegel and Bryson 2016).

Respond or React?

The ability to respond rather than react during challenging interactions requires continued connection and the use of skilled social engagement strategies. Positive social engagement emphasizes setting and maintaining appropriate boundaries and monitoring the way we present our ideas and our requests. Healthy engagement highlights shared goals, like managing difficulties from a win-win perspective, safeguarding personal integrity, and prioritizing relationships over being right.

Responding versus Reacting

When one reactive brain meets another reactive brain, there is bound to be trouble. The interaction becomes a "life or death" struggle that reinforces ongoing negative social engagement patterns (Badenoch 2008).

Become a social engagement master. Assess your engagement skills, resolve any weaknesses, and learn to respond rather than react.

The pull of entrainment is strong, and responding rather than reacting requires a significant amount of energy and resolve. An adult's countenance and demeanor must remain at least neutral. To manage negative contagion, we need to stay connected, respectful, and engaged. It is helpful to pause, review regulation strategies, reconceptualize the interaction, and consider ways to manage things differently (Church 2018).

During stressful interactions, choose language wisely. Words have the capacity to empower or disempower, connect or disconnect, accept or reject. Remember that some children have been harmed while being compliant. Be sensitive and avoid using language that emphasizes power differentials or that triggers resistance or disconnection.

Be willing to modify your message in order to decrease reactivity. This accommodation draws on the regulation benefits inherent in the social engagement system and becomes a model for co-regulation. With care, and even while addressing problem behaviors, we can influence a child's emotional state, limit escalation, and save the relationship for skill-building and future bonding. When we resist the pull to reenact destructive patterns, we create a new possibility.

Main Ideas

Humans are hard-wired to connect, and healthy relationships become foundations for growth and resilience. Just as it negatively impacts the developing vertical and horizontal brain, toxic stress damages the social engagement system. When this happens, connecting with others becomes painful or dangerous, rather than a source of comfort and support.

Emotional contagion means that my dysregulation may become your dysregulation. Fortunately, an attuned interaction can facilitate a corrective experience. Corrective experiences offer remediation and help people communicate and work together in spite of long-standing destructive engagement patterns.

The ability to respond rather than react during a difficult encounter demands that a person stay regulated. This requires significant skill, control, and presence. A regulated and responsive stance highlights connection, and thus ensures the best outcome even in highly-charged interactions.

Reader Reflection

The need for nurturance and connection is hard-wired in each of us. Unfortunately, adverse early experiences can derail interactional skills and damage the ability to ask for help and to locate and utilize healthy social resources.

- How can connection help children downregulate?
- Can you remember a time when you were either positively or negatively "entrained" by another person?

Recall your problematic student or situation and consider the following.

- How would you characterize the relationships or interactions?
- What social strengths or weaknesses affect the outcome?
- Is there a corrective experience that might be helpful?

Social Engagement and Conflict

Staying regulated increases your ability to turn on reciprocal positive social engagement. Remaining connected is key to this possibility.

When dealing with upsetting issues or conflict, activate upper brain circuits, create a holding space, use reflective listening, and encourage collaboration.

CHAPTER 9

SOCIAL ENGAGEMENT ACTIVITIES AND EXPERIENCES: RESPONDING VERSUS REACTING, CO-REGULATION, AND SOCIAL EMOTIONAL LEARNING (SEL)

Positive social engagement becomes a regulation pathway that can limit reactivity, strengthen resilience, and develop the skills that maintain healthy relationships. We are social beings who regulate one another through our interactions. When we share corrective experiences that help children recover from destructive patterns, we use our co-regulatory capacities for everyone's greatest good.

Social Engagement Goals

Recognize: We are constantly co-regulating; I choose to manage my impact on others.

Empathize: Toxic stress can derail a child's capacity to engage with others in healthy ways.

Know: My personal engagement patterns may set me up to react rather than respond.

Resource: I connect and help everyone feel accepted.

This section has activities, experiences, and resources to help the reader identify and monitor social engagement patterns, build healthy social strategies, and continue to strengthen emotional intelligence. Some exercises are psychoeducational and focus on ways to stay responsive during difficult exchanges. Other activities explore the critical role that language plays in helping children downregulate. There is a brief introduction to attachment styles and their influence on relationship-building.

Social and emotional learning (SEL) programs and methods are becoming an integral part of the education curriculum. The goal of SEL is to help children learn, practice, and deepen basic social skills that are vital for school, work, and life success. The relationship between emotional intelligence and empathy is another area of focus.

Any of the activities presented can be expanded or modified in ways that are most effective and helpful to the reader. See Chapter 3 for the movement, mindfulness, and energy exercises that may also be beneficial for this pathway.

Activity: Responsive versus Reactive

When things are going well, it is easy to be calm, empathetic, and regulated. The brain is in a responsive state, we feel relaxed and positive, and we are better able to connect and manage difficult situations. Everything changes the instant we become distressed or feel threatened. We shift into survival mode, move into reactivity, and are more prone to act out, discharge negativity, and resort to old, destructive patterns.

It is helpful to become aware of what it is like when we are responsive versus reactive, and to understand how these states affect the quality of our interactions. By learning to differentiate between the two states, we are better able to track and manage ourselves in the moment and it becomes easier to stay regulated regardless of how others act.

Below are some of the qualities, attributes, and characteristics that are typical for each state.

Responsive Brain

- Greater present moment awareness
- Accurate social appraisal
- Access to social engagement strategies
- Ability to downregulate quickly

Reactive Brain

- Default to old projections or negative beliefs
- Easily triggered stress response
- Susceptible to emotional contagion
- Increased dysregulation

Consider how each of the above impacts how well you stay connected.

Think of someone with whom you often become reactive. Reflect on the characteristics listed above and create an action plan.

Activity: Relate and Downregulate

Challenging behaviors, like disrespect or noncompliance, trigger our default settings, and prime us for unconscious social conditioning. At these moments, it is imperative to access the tools that return us to responsive states and help us downregulate. Social engagement resources help us stay connected and be more able to de-escalate tough interactions.

Connection is like a superpower with which we relate in order to downregulate. When we prioritize a respectful tone and message, we optimize an experience that calms and boosts cooperation. By being receptive, respectful, and connected, it is easier for everyone keep his or her balance and build a healthy relationship.

Below are ways to relate and downregulate.

- Breathe mindfully. Without straining, extend the exhalation phase of the breath cycle. This engages the parasympathetic nervous system and helps calm the body.

- Attend to what is happening in the present moment without judgment. Check your level of commitment to stay connected, no matter what. Remind yourself of the benefits of modeling positive engagement.

- Stay grounded. Feel your feet on the floor and make an effort to remain fully in your body.

- Review a previous success, or reaffirm your intention to show your best self in every way you interact and communicate.

- When things become tense, invite everyone to take a breath or a break. If you have become reactive, pause. Apologize. Do not worry about having made a mistake. Repairs are relationship builders.

When we connect emotionally before we address problem behavior, we influence emotional states, limit escalation, decrease physical and emotional distress, and safeguard the relationship.

Practice up-leveling your relational strategies. Notice any differences in the quality or outcome of your interactions.

Activity: Co-Regulation

We are social beings, constantly responding to subtle informational cues that are below our awareness thresholds. These cues help us predict another person's state of mind and likely behavior. The cues also influence our own emotional states and regulation. One person's autonomic nervous system interacts with another person's system, for better or worse. This process has been compared to contagion because my dysregulation can become your dysregulation.

Another way to understand what is happening in our interactions is to acknowledge that humans act as co-regulators. Co-regulation is a natural part of the psychobiological interconnection that occurs with social connection. We affect one another through our relationships. It is possible to use this co-regulatory capacity intentionally to facilitate regulation and well-being in others.

Consider the following.

- Compare a model of contagion with co-regulation. What are the differences? Which feels most useful for you?

Assertiveness and setting clear boundaries protect us from other's negative emotions.

- Do you use strategies to maintain healthy emotional and behavioral boundaries? Are there areas that need strengthening?

- How do you support yourself when surrounded by negative emotions?

- Think of a challenging relationship. If you were to imagine yourself as a material substance, what would it be? For example, are you "porous" or "impermeable" to others? How does this material help you stay regulated?

By embodying positive emotional states, we can intentionally influence another person's health and well-being.

- Think of ways to use art, role-playing, demonstrations, or other techniques to practice positive entrainment with children.

Activity: Word Power

Authoritative language that is respectful and collaborative both connects and communicates. Making a request in a way that feels warm yet authoritative optimizes regulation for both parties. Language reflects our thinking, shapes our sense of self, and influences how well our messages are received (Denton 2013). Children with significant trauma histories can be triggered by normal requests that are only meant to guide behavior and learning.

Authoritative language is distinct from authoritarian language, which has a strong base in power. Authoritarian communication styles include phrases that come across as commands and demands. This style is likely to activate defensive circuits that increase reactivity. Those who have been harmed while being compliant are particularly vulnerable. They are often sensitized to language that accentuates power differences.

Word choice conveys overt and covert messages. A strong "No!" or a precision command is essential when real danger is present. We do not negotiate or connect in front of an oncoming car. However, in many situations, and particularly with children who are easily dysregulated, an authoritarian style is problematic (Jensen 2013).

- When making a request, avoid demanding or using sarcastic language. If a child is slow to comply, try planned ignoring. Let the child know that you notice his or her behavior, then let it go and move on.

- Give a direction, make expectations clear, and stay connected. If compliance does not follow, discuss it later when both you and the child are more available and regulated. Use a solution-focused approach and brainstorm alternatives like being able to move, substitute activities, or take a break.

- Acknowledge when things are not going well. You might use a statement like, "This isn't going in a great direction, so let's take a break and figure out a better way later." Or you could try, "Whoops, we're getting off track. Let's breathe for a minute."

Connecting statements initially sound strange, but come more easily with time. Instead of "Sit!" you might try, "I can see it's hard for you to stay in your seat right now, but please be seated."

With practice, authoritative language becomes more accessible in the moment. Do not worry about making mistakes. When we own our limitations, we model ways of being together that strengthen our authority and connection.

Activity: Conversation Connects

The social brain develops through relationship. By talking together, we discover what we think, who we are, and how we belong. Meaningful conversation is an art form that requires complex skills, like being able to listen, to share and take turns, to trust others to respond, and to interpret non-verbal information. Conversation that cultivates connection can make a profound difference in a child's confidence and self-worth.

To begin a great conversation, check to see if you are feeling present and responsive. Then make sure it is a good time to talk. Mundane questions can be disconnecting so be creative. Children often meet the question, "How was your day?" with a routine response that feels detached or disengaged. Stimulate enthusiasm by asking a novel question that requires a personal touch.

- In lieu of asking how the day went, ask for one highlight or lowlight from the day.

- Focus on the unusual. Try something like, "Tell me one kindness, or one surprise from your day."

- Capture the imagination by asking what a "perfect day" might look like.

- Describe the day from a favorite character's perspective.

Use intentional techniques like compelling questions or engineered controversy to generate a meaningful discussion. These processes highlight skills like respectfully managing differences and expressing difficult feelings (Jensen 2005).

- Choose a major world problem. How would you go about solving it? What do you need to begin?

In groups, formalized procedures like using a timer or talking stick create structure.

- A talking stick can be any object that the designated speaker holds. It signifies that only this person is allowed to speak. When the person finishes, he or she passes the stick to the next person. Have the group decide beforehand whether individuals can comment on what others have shared.

- Set a timer for each turn. Decide beforehand whether members must address a particular topic, may choose their own topic, or may choose to pass.

Activity: Attachment Awareness

Attachment is the deep and enduring emotional bond that connects people across time and space. Earliest caregiver experiences shape the attachments that become the foundations for our social engagement. These attachment experiences generate patterns that significantly impact the ability to form and maintain relationships throughout one's lifetime.

Research has identified a number of basic attachment styles. Each attachment style reflects a set of beliefs about self, others, and the world. Attachment style affects how we learn about ourselves, get along with others, and function in society (Wallin 2007). Attachment styles are commonly labeled secure or insecure. Insecure attachment is further subdivided into categories like anxious, avoidant, and disorganized.

- Secure attachment is characterized by interactions that are positive, pro-social, and reciprocal. A person with secure attachment believes that his or her needs will be met, and he or she has access to many effective social engagement strategies.

- Insecure attachment is based in the belief that others will not or cannot meet the individual's needs. People with insecure attachment styles have chronic dysfunctional ways of relating to others and resulting decreased resilience. They often employ limited and ineffective social engagement strategies.

Attachment styles develop early, but there is growing evidence that these patterns can change during the lifetime. It is possible to "earn" a secure attachment base with social repair and remediation, such as through corrective experiences.

Explore any books or articles on attachment theory that are appealing to you. Consider the way attachment history influences the relationships around you.

- Do you have a sense of your own attachment style? How does your attachment affect the social strategies you use?

- Are attachment issues a factor in your previously identified problematic situation or in any relationships?

Activity: Engagement Shields

Being isolated or outcast creates social pain that undermines physical and mental health, learning potential, and emotional well-being. Feelings of exclusion or rejection are particularly problematic for adolescents. Social connection, on the other hand, increases motivation and achievement, and creates a "shield" against anxiety and depression (Jensen 2013).

- Create a social engagement shield using art materials or a computer graphics program. The banner might celebrate personal connections, strengths, and resources, such as friends and family, hobbies and interests, clubs, associations, and other affiliations.

- Share the shield with a partner, the class, or community.

Create a discussion forum for peers and colleagues to consider the connection opportunities available in your school or community.

- Identify social strengths and resources that are available for students and staff. Brainstorm connection challenges and share solutions and successes.

- Discuss the connection opportunities open to vulnerable children, especially those who are marginalized or impoverished.

- Investigate SEL (Social Emotional Learning) projects, common interest groups, volunteer positions, before- and after-school leadership opportunities, and cooperative learning. Develop and adopt school and system-wide tools and traditions for promoting acceptance, inclusion, and positivity.

Activity: Social and Emotional Learning (SEL)

Social and emotional learning (SEL) is a category of programs and methods aimed at helping children and young adults develop social, emotional, behavioral, and character skills. Social and emotional learning programs explicitly teach or remediate these skills. SEL methods are designed to support healthy relationships and citizenship for individuals in schools and the workplace.

Social and emotional skills develop from infancy, and, according to social cognitive neuroscientists, these skills derive from modeling that happens during early interactions. When a soothing adult is not available during stressful circumstances, a child feels a real loss that influences his or her social patterns far into the future (Lieberman and Van Horn 2011). Fortunately, social and emotional skills can be addressed by directed educational experiences aimed at acquisition and mastery.

SEL programs target discrete areas like cooperation, responsible decision-making, and managing strong emotions. Other skill areas include learning to recognize emotions in oneself and others, developing empathy, and using clear and assertive communication (Merrell 2008). SEL categories can be broad, like cognitive regulation, emotional processing, and character-building. Goals can also be as simple as learning to deal with anger or letting go of stress.

Explore the SEL literature and find programs that are interesting and age-appropriate. SEL takes place in formal and informal settings, such as classrooms or counseling offices. Try using a formalized program or adapt a structured program lesson to an informal setting by taking a walk together, playing a game, or crafting a project (Phifer and Sibbald 2017).

Activity: Empathy and EQ

Empathy, the ability to share another's feelings and perspectives, is an indicator of healthy development. When we feel into another person's experience and situation, we have the opportunity to enrich understanding, increase acceptance, and develop tolerance. Exercises that strengthen interpersonal awareness and perspective-taking support empathy and develop emotional intelligence.

Although toxic stress often leads to empathy failure, we can address developmental deficits with activities that increase empathic capacity (Goleman 2006). Self-awareness is a starting point for social and emotional intelligence. To foster self-awareness, have the individual pay attention to his or her thoughts, feelings, and experiences.

- How did you know what you were feeling?
- What else makes you feel that way?
- What makes things feel better, worse, or easier?

Perspective-taking also builds empathic response.

- Why do you think that baby was laughing or crying?
- That man sounded upset or sad. What might have happened?
- What else could they have thought, said, or done?

Empathy activities and games can be as simple as pretending to be someone else. Role-play different characters from books or films and imagine their thoughts, feelings, and beliefs.

- How would this character react to _____?
- What would he or she do next?

CHAPTER 10

THE ART AND SCIENCE OF REGULATION

Self-regulation is a foundation for success and well-being. Regulation skills play a role in whether we can feel secure, actualize our potential, and connect with others. Dysregulation, on the other hand, derails individual success, takes a toll on educational systems and public safety, and impacts the health of society as a whole. This book has examined how brain systems and their pathways support or limit regulatory capacity, and offered exercises, activities, and practices to strengthen skill mastery.

Using a science-practice format, we examined common factors in dysregulation patterns and outlined a model of inquiry to guide the intervention process. The model focused on three brain systems which become regulation pathways. The pathway model provides a perspective to demystify troublesome behaviors and capitalize on the brain's capacity to move toward health and wholeness.

Core Ideas

- Regulation affects how we manage energy, emotion, attention, and behavior.
- Toxic stress plays a significant role in the development of regulation skill deficits.
- Unmet needs and reactivity often drive dysregulated states.
- Dysregulated coping can cause chronic, destructive habit patterns.
- Brain science offers evidence that behavior change is possible and can be targeted.
- Keeping calm, respecting differences, and staying connected enhances regulation in self and others.
- Brain states are contagious and we act as co-regulators for one another.

Looking Back

There are several ideas that deserve review. The impact of toxic stress on a child's life cannot be overemphasized. Toxic stress influences nearly every aspect of early brain development and negatively impacts critical growth and functioning. The results are a chronic stress response activation that permanently affects emotional and behavioral default settings. By learning to identify the effects of toxic stress, it is possible to conceptualize a child's behavior from a place of neutrality and to respond effectively and with greater compassion.

A regulation pathway model guides how adults perceive, interpret, and respond to problematic behavior. The model acts as a matrix to organize both self and others during moments of crisis. When a child's unmet needs are taken into account, the adult can clarify the function of the behavior, identify a pathway, and choose appropriate effective strategies and interventions.

Implementing the pathway model requires that the reader engages in reflection and introspection. Brain-trained educators and specialists check their personal default brain states, stress response settings, learning biases, and social-engagement patterns and resources. They notice their body and brain states, and are curious about their own early developmental patterns. These scientist practitioners are familiar with personal triggers and can respond rather than react. They make relational repairs and act as change agents in order to avoid burnout.

Humans are multidimensional and complex. From this vantage point, effective interventions are derived from science to storytelling, art to engineering, mythology to technology. Regulation tools take this into account by attempting to access and address the many facets of the human condition.

Looking Beyond

A final question asks how these materials can be of most use. For professionals dealing with serious dysregulation issues, the pathway model may be particularly helpful. The model provides a structure for determining

- which brain system may be activated;

- how unmet needs and reactivity are implicated in decreased regulatory control; and
- which interventions may be most effective for increasing regulation.

The model moves the inquiry from a rote take on behavior to a dynamic consideration of how the regulation skills of all participants influence the outcome.

For readers who are already brain-trained, the activities chapters may be most useful. Many of the exercises and resources are meant to inspire the reader's personal creativity and any experience can be adapted and improvised to fit the current situation.

The book may be especially valuable for educators and other specialists who can make a significant contribution by bringing brain-based techniques into educational settings and by sharing these science-based materials and practices with colleagues and friends. A shared perspective creates a foundation beyond the fear and dismissal that dysregulated children often evoke in others. The vision can become less about children who are failing or who are being failed by a system, and more about a professional community serving difficult children through informed practices.

These materials were written as a resource and a support, meant to renew the reader's own vision and sense of possibility. Behavior makes perfect sense given what the brain and body have learned. Fortunately, there is a capacity to recover and grow, to reach potentials higher than imagined, and maybe higher than anyone imagined for us. This is the message that can be shared with one other and with those children whose lives you touch.

Vertical Integration and the Stress Response

- Does the child feel safe and secure?
- Is the adult aware of environmental threats and the effects of toxic stress?
- Can the adult recognize his or her own personal stress responses?
- Are the messages, "You are safe," and "I am calm?"

Specialization and the Horizontal Brain

- Does the child feel appreciated, valid, and seen?
- Does the adult make sure no one is marginalized, made to feel different, inferior, or less-than?
- Can the adult manage his or her personal strengths, weaknesses, and biases?
- Are the messages "I acknowledge you," and "I see and value your difference?"

Engagement and the Social Brain

- Does the child feel he or she belongs and is accepted?
- Does the adult monitor cohesiveness, bullying, and alienation?
- Can the adult show warmth and affiliate with the group?
- Are the messages "You are not alone," and "I accept and connect with you?"

REFERENCES

Armstrong, Steven J., Eva Cools, and Eugene Sadler-Smith. 2012. "Role of cognitive styles in business and management: Reviewing 40 years of research." *International Journal of Management Reviews* 14, no. 3 (June): 238–262.

Badenoch, Bonnie. 2008. *Being a Brain-Wise Therapist: A Practical Guide to Interpersonal Neurobiology,* Norton Series on Interpersonal Neurobiology, edited by Allen N. Schore. W.W. Norton & Company.

Bashant, Jennifer L. 2020. *Building a Trauma-Informed Compassionate Classroom: Strategies to Reduce Challenging Behavior, Improve Learning Outcomes and Increase Student Engagement.* PESI Publishing & Media.

Belmont, Judith A. 2006. *103 Group Activities and Treatment Ideas & Practical Strategies.* PESI Publishing & Media.

Blaustein, Margaret, and Kristine M. Kinniburgh. 2019. *Treating Traumatic Stress in Children and Adolescent: How to Foster Resilience through Attachment, Self-Regulation, and Competency.* Guilford Press.

Bruin, Esther I. de, Bonne J. H. Zijlstra and Susan M. Bögels. 2013. "The Meaning of Mindfulness in Children and Adolescents: Further Validation of the Child and Adolescent Mindfulness Measure (CAMM) in Two Independent Samples from The Netherlands." Mindfulness 5, no. 4: 422-430.

Center on the Developing Child at Harvard University. "Experiences Build Brain Architecture." Accessed December 14, 2015. https://developingchild.harvard.edu.

Church, Dawson. 2015. *Psychological Trauma: Healing Its Roots in Brain, Body, and Memory.* Energy Psychology Press.

———. 2018. *Mind to Matter: The Astonishing Science of How Your Brain Creates Material Reality*. Hay House, Inc.

Curwin, Richard L., Allen N. Mendler, and Brian D. Mendler. 2008. *Discipline with Dignity, 4th Edition: How to Build Responsibility, Relationships, and Respect in Your Classroom*. ASCD.

Davidson, Richard J., Jon Kabat-Zinn, Jessica Schumacher, Melissa A. Rosenkranz, Daniel Muller, Saki F. Santorelli, Ferris Urbanowski, Anne Harrington, Katherine A. Bonus and John F. Sheridan. 2003. "Alterations in Brain and Immune Function Produced by Mindfulness Meditation." *Psychosomatic Medicine* 65, no. 4: 564–570.

Delahooke, Mona. 2019. *Beyond Behaviors: Using Brain Science and Compassion to Understand and Solve Children's Behavioral Challenges*. PESI Publishing & Media.

Denton, Paula. 2015. *The Power of Our Words: Teacher Language That Helps Children Learn*. Center For Responsive Schools, Inc.

Eden, Donna, and Dondi Dahlin. 2012. *The Little Book of Energy Medicine*. Penguin Books.

Eden, Donna, and David Feinstein. 2008. *Energy Medicine*. Penguin Books.

Ekman, Paul. 2003. *Emotions Revealed: Recognizing Faces and Feelings to Improve Communication and Emotional Life*. Henry Holt & Company.

Feinstein, David. 2004. *Energy Psychology Interactive: Rapid Interventions for Lasting Change*. Innersource.

———. 2023. "Integrating the Manual Stimulation of Acupuncture Points into Psychotherapy: A Systematic Review with Clinical Recommendations." *Journal of Psychotherapy Integration* 33, no. 1: 47–67.

Feinstein, David, Donna Eden, and Gary Craig. 2005. *The Promise of Energy*

Psychology: Revolutionary Tools for Dramatic Personal Change. Penguin Books.

Feinstein, David, and Stanley Krippner. 1997. *The Mythic Path: Discovering the Guiding Stories of Your Past--Creating a Vision of Your Future*. G.P. Putnam's Sons.

Felitti, Vincent J., Robert F. Anda, Dale Nordenberg, David F. Williamson, Alison M. Spitz, Valerie Edwards, Mary P. Koss, and James S. Marks. 1998. "Relationship of Childhood Abuse and Household Dysfunction to Many of the Leading Causes of Death in Adults." *American Journal of Preventive Medicine* 14, no. 4: 245–58.

Fisher, Janina. 2017. *Healing the Fragmented Selves of Trauma Survivors: Overcoming Internal Self-Alienation*. Routledge.

Garland, Teresa. 2014. *Self-Regulation Interventions and Strategies: Keeping the Body, Mind and Emotions on Task in Children with Autism, ADHD or Sensory Disorders*. PESI Publishing & Media.

Goleman, Daniel, Bstan-'dzin-Rgya-Mtsho, Dalai Lama Xiv, and Richard J. Davidson. 2004. *Destructive Emotions: How Can We Overcome Them? A Scientific Dialogue with the Dalai Lama*. Bantam Books.

Hahn, Thich Nhat. 2011. *Planting Seeds: Practicing Mindfulness with Children*. Parallax Press.

Hölzel, Britta K., James Carmody, Karleyton C. Evans, Elizabeth A. Hoge, Jeffery A. Dusek, Lucas Morgan, Roger K. Pitman, and Sara W. Lazar. 2009. "Stress Reduction Correlates with Structural Changes in the Amygdala." *Social Cognitive and Affective Neuroscience* 5, no. 1: 11–17.

Hubert, Bill. 2014. *Bal-A-Vis-X: Rhythmic Balance/Auditory/Vision Exercises for Brain and Brain-Body Integration*. Bal-A-Vis-X, Inc.

Jäncke, Lutz. 2009. "Music drives brain plasticity." *F1000 Biology Reports,* 1.

Jensen, Eric. 2005. *Teaching with the Brain in Mind*. ASCD.

———. 2009. *Teaching with Poverty in Mind: What Being Poor Does to Kids' Brains and What Schools Can Do about It*. ASCD.

———. 2013. *Engaging Students with Poverty in Mind: Practical Strategies for Raising Achievement*. ASCD.

Kabat-Zinn, Jon. 1994. *Wherever You Go, There You Are: Mindfulness Meditation in Everyday Life*. Hyperion.

Kenney, Lynne, and Wendy Young. 2015. *Bloom: 50 Things to Say, Think and Do with Anxious, Angry, and Over-The-Top Kids*. Unhooked Books.

Kindlon, Daniel J., Michael Thompson, and Teresa Barker. 2000. *Raising Cain: Protecting the Emotional Life of Boys*. Ballantine Books.

Koontz, Suzy. "Official Website of Suzy Koontz, Founder and CEO of Math & Movement." Accessed June 2, 2019. https://suzykoontz.com.

Lieberman, Alicia F., and Patricia Van Horn. 2008. *Psychotherapy with Infants and Young Children: Repairing the Effects of Stress and Trauma on Early Attachment*. Guilford Press.

Madigan, J. B. "Action Based Learning." Accessed May 14, 2018. Actionbasedlearning. https://www.abllab.com.

Mendoza, Krystyne, and Loretta Bradley. 2020. "Using Storytelling for Counseling with Children Who Have Experienced Trauma." *Journal of Mental Health Counseling* 43, no. 1: 1–18.

Merrell, Kenneth W. 2013. *Helping Students Overcome Depression and Anxiety, Second Edition*. Guilford Press.

National Institute for the Clinical Application of Behavioral Medicine. "How Anger Affects Your Brain and Body." NICABM Psychotherapy Infographic. Accessed June 12, 2018. https://www.nicabm.com.

Ogden, Pat, and Janina Fisher. 2015. *Sensorimotor Psychotherapy: Interventions for Trauma and Attachment.* W.W. Norton & Company.

Ogden, Pat, and Kekuni Minton. 2000. "Sensorimotor Psychotherapy: One Method for Processing Traumatic Memory." *Traumatology* 6, no. 3: 149–73.

Ogden, Pat, Kekuni Minton, and Clare Pain. 2006. *Trauma and the Body: A Sensorimotor Approach to Psychotherapy.* W.W. Norton & Company.

Peterson, Jordan. 1999. *Maps of Meaning: The Architecture of Belief.* Routledge.

Phifer, Lisa Weed, Amanda K. Crowder, and Tracy Elsenratt. 2017. *CBT Toolbox for Children and Adolescents: Over 200 Worksheets & Exercises for Trauma, ADHD, Autism, Anxiety, Depression & Conduct Disorders.* PESI Publishing & Media.

Phifer, Lisa Weed, and Laura Sibbald. 2020. *Trauma-Informed Social-Emotional Toolbox for Children and Adolescents: 116 Worksheets and Skill-Building Exercises to Support Safety, Connection and Empowerment.* PESI Publishing & Media.

Porges, Stephen W. 2011. *The Polyvagal Theory: Neurophysiological Foundations of Emotions, Attachment, Communication, and Self-Regulation.* W. W. Norton & Company.

Rakesh, Divyangana, and Sarah Whittle. 2021. "Socioeconomic Status and the Developing Brain – a Systematic Review of Neuroimaging Findings in Youth." *Neuroscience & Biobehavioral Reviews* 130: 379–407.

Ratey, John J., and James Loehr, 2011. "The positive impact of physical activity on cognition during adulthood: a review of underlying mechanisms, evidence and recommendations." 22, no. 2: 171-185. https://doi.org/10.1515/rns.2011.017.

Rauscher, Frances, Gordon Shaw, Linda Levine, Eric Wright, Wendy Dennis, and Robert Newcomb. 1997. "Music Training Causes Long-Term Enhancement of Preschool Children's Spatial–Temporal Reasoning." *Neurological Research* 19, no 1: 2–8.

Schore, Allan N. 2015. *Affect Regulation and the Origin of the Self.* Routledge.

Schreiber, Darren, Greg Fonzo, Alan N. Simmons, Christopher T. Dawes, Taru Flagan, James H. Fowler, and Martin P. Paulus. 2013. "Red brain, blue brain: Evaluative processes differ in Democrats and Republicans." *PLoS one* 8, no. 2: e52970.

Seligman, Martin E. P. 2002. *Authentic Happiness: Using the New Positive Psychology to Realize Your Potential for Lasting Fulfilment.* Simon and Schuster.

———. 2006. *Learned Optimism: How to Change Your Mind and Your Life.* Vintage Books.

Shapiro, Francine. 2018. *Eye Movement Desensitization and Reprocessing (EMDR) Therapy: Basic Principles, Protocols, and Procedures.* Guilford Press.

Siegel, Daniel J. 2007. *The Mindful Brain: Reflection and Attunement in the Cultivation of Well-Being.* W.W. Norton & Company.

———. 2012. *The Developing Mind: Toward a Neurobiology of Interpersonal Experience.* Guilford Press.

Siegel, Daniel J., and Tina Payne Bryson. 2011. *The Whole-Brain Child: 12 Revolutionary Strategies to Nurture Your Child's Developing Mind.* Delacorte Press.

———. 2016. *No-Drama Discipline: The Whole-Brain Way to Calm the Chaos and Nurture Your Child's Developing Mind.* Bantam Books.

Snel, Eline. 2013. *Sitting Still like a Frog: Mindfulness Exercises for Kids (and Their Parents).* Shambhala.

Soutar, Richard, and Robert Longo. 2011. *Doing Neurofeedback: An Introduction.* ISNR Research Foundation.

Stien, Phyllis, and Joshua C. Kendall. 2014. *Psychological Trauma and the Developing Brain: Neurologically Based Interventions for Troubled Children*. Routledge.

Van der Kolk, Bessel. 2015. *The Body Keeps the Score: Brain, Mind, and Body in the Healing of Trauma*. Penguin Books.

Walker, Lauren. 2014. *Energy Medicine Yoga: Amplify the Healing Power of Your Yoga Practice*. Sounds True.

Wallin, David J. 2007. *Attachment in Psychotherapy*. Guildford Press.

Whitaker, Todd. 2015. *What Great Principals Do Differently: Eighteen Things That Matter Most*. Routledge.

ACKNOWLEDGMENTS

I have many people to thank and much to be grateful for. I send sincere gratitude to the following people who made this book possible.

In my early years as an educator, Geneve Geer, Aaron P. Dye, and Judy Rule provided critical guidance and opportunities for leadership and development. Their mastery, vision, and commitment to children were a constant inspiration.

My students and patients, although I can't mention you by name, taught me most of what I know, and it has been an honor to work and learn together.

BYU colleagues Erin and Reed Mueller and professors Allen Bergin, Brent Slife, and Gary Burlingame shared their friendship, support, and brilliance, and made those five years a touchstone for inquiry and personal excellence.

Friends and colleagues Heather MacDonald and Lauren Maxim generously listened to me think and talk through this project, always welcomed a discussion, and gave essential and thoughtful feedback at critical times.

Alaska teammates, Suzie Michaud and Jessa Comer looked beyond the behavior to a child's worth and dignity and made it their business to give every kid a fair chance. Thank you for my home away from home. Liz Baer, my editor provided consistent and skilled feedback.

Family Girl Power, sisters Kathleen Sutcliffe and Gail Marnik, and nieces Fiona and Miranda Marnik-Said supported me with their unique gifts and accomplishments. They continue to show up to make the world a better place. My husband Steve offered endless encouragement and gave me all the time I needed.

Finally, I send my gratitude to my mother, Mathilda Frances Sanders. Her love has been a source of strength and among my greatest treasures.

Printed in the United States
by Baker & Taylor Publisher Services